RISJ *CHALLENGES*

What's happening to our news

An investigation into the likely impact of the digital
revolution on the economics of news publishing in the UK

Andrew Currah

REUTERS
INSTITUTE for the
STUDY of
JOURNALISM

Contents

Foreword

by Mandy Cormack, a director of the Joseph Rowntree Reform Trust

The Joseph Rowntree Reform Trust has, since its inception, taken an interest in supporting press and broadcasting freedom, and in particular the protection of the public service ethic. Both principles have a central role in the functioning of a democratic state, providing citizens with the information on which to participate in the democratic process and holding those in authority to account for their actions and omissions. At the heart of this is the news-making process—the agenda shaping, gathering and distribution of news about politics, society and the economy, and the world in which we live.

In May 2007, the Reuters Institute for the Study of Journalism hosted a workshop 'Money and News' sponsored by the Joseph Rowntree Reform Trust. The purpose of the workshop was to explore the impact of the media's commercial operation on the conduct of its democratic news-making role in the twenty-first century. By looking at how value is created through the entire chain of activities of a modern news media organisation, the aim was to disaggregate the process and take a fresh look at each stage as well as to examine the drivers and constraints on overall performance and how they impacted the functioning of the media in our democracy today. The outcome of the workshop was the remit for this research project.

Like many industries, the media industry is experiencing specialisation and the outsourcing of non-core activities, as well as change driven by new technology and an increasingly international operating environment. The disaggregation of the value chain of news production put the spotlight on three core steps in the process: newsgathering, news processing and news distribution. Newsgathering has seen a growth in the public relations industry handling the provision of inputs to the news media, with increasingly sophisticated norms of operation, paid for by clients. Advances in technology, in particular, in internet and digitally based communications, are revolutionising both the processing and distribution of news as well as how web-literate consumers access news. These changes are challenging the traditional economic model of consolidated advertising and subscriptions that has underpinned the development of a cadre of professional journalists.

This report explores these changes. In an industry where information is the lifeblood of its activities, it has been at times difficult to obtain the level of detailed data to substantiate all aspects of the research enquiries. Nevertheless, through interviews with those at the front line and the analysis of industry and company specific data, the researchers have prepared a report which demonstrates the level of change that is taking place. The scale of the change challenges many of the old certainties and underlines the importance of a wide-ranging debate on the implications of what is going on for democratic participation in the governance of the UK. The opportunities to increase democratic engagement will challenge all parties—from the media and from the political world—to approach the realities of the new media world with an open mind. This report is offered, not as an answer, but as a contribution to that open debate.

Thank you to the many individuals who have been generous in their time and willingness to share their understanding of the events that are unfolding. Thanks are especially due to the expert reference group, to the team who have steered it through (John Lloyd, Geert Linnebank and David Ure) and to the indefatigable enthusiasm of the report's author Andrew Currah and the researchers Harriet Cullinan and Kirsten Westlake.

Foreword

By Tim Gardam, Chair of the Steering Committee
Reuters Institute for the Study of Journalism

The age of digital media has brought with it evangelists and cassandras in equal measure. There have never been so many sources of news available to us, as the distinctions between text, video and sound break down and technologies converge. No commercial news organisation can afford to ignore the online market, but equally it is unclear how any will be able to profit from it.

There are two points at issue: what is the future business model for commercial news gathering, and, more fundamentally, what is the future for professional journalism when the price of information has in many places dropped to zero? News today is ambient and access to news is free. Anyone in the blogosphere can claim the title of journalist. For all those who acclaim the worldwide web as the greatest force for freedom of expression ever created, there are those who look with foreboding at a media culture where the polyphony of self-appointed reporters and commentators drown out the reasoned voices of editorially disciplined argument and professional reporting.

What is beyond dispute is that the basis of journalism as a transaction, where in the past the many have paid to gain access to the writings of the few, has changed fundamentally. In an age of real time information, and limitless distraction, journalists can no longer assume that their 'professionalism' has a secure value. Yet it remains hard to imagine a civil society that functions effectively, or a citizenry that can hold its government democratically to account, without a self-confident independent media with a professional ethic that ascribes to itself standards, however hotly these are disputed.

The Reuters Institute for the Study of Journalism was established at Oxford University in order to examine the interaction between journalism and society and the implications of its changing nature. In the past, much debate has been centred on journalism's principles and ethics and the proper relationship between journalists and those in power. However, in recent years, those arguments have been increasingly overshadowed by a prior economic concern—the revolution in business models brought about by the web which is calling into question the basis of journalism as a profession. 'What's happening to our news' is therefore not a rhetorical question but a harder edged examination of the economics of news reporting.

This report has set out to address issues that may be simple to define yet where the evidence is hard to establish: how news organisations now spend their money and the nature of the editorial decisions they take as they respond to the logic of the internet. The author, Andrew Currah, supported by a team of advisors, demonstrates the consequences of the internet economy; it sucks advertising revenues from the old media platforms that created news content to the new media platforms that simply aggregate it, thus threatening to 'hollow out the craft of journalism'. The modern journalism does not so much encounter stories in the real world as segment and adapt them to the virtual world of multi platform real time media. The role and judgement of the editor is also called into question in a market where the clickstream demonstrates mercilessly the popularity of particular individual stories. It is not that news is disappearing in the age of the web —quite the opposite—but what news becomes has changed.

'What's happening to our news' is not content simply to rest on the question it poses. As with all the publications in the Reuters Institute 'Challenges' series, it lays out recommendations for remedies, proposals that take the argument into the terrain of regulation and to questions surrounding the public and private funding of news. This report is an important contribution to the study of the future of journalism in the online age; its empirical approach has unpicked a systemic problem that will not go away. It is a topic that the Reuters Institute intends to develop and explore in the months ahead.

Summary

(1) 'What's happening to our news' investigates the shifting economic foundations of print and television national news in the UK—and specifically, the impact of such shifts on the quality, independence, diversity and civic value of British journalism. The report is based on a year of research, including over 70 interviews with senior participants in the UK news media.

(2) The principal conclusion is that increasing commercial pressure, mainly driven by the inherent characteristics of the digital revolution, is undermining the business models that pay for the news (apart from BBC news, which is funded by the licence fee). In our view, this will weaken some media organisations, threaten to hollow out the craft of journalism and adversely impact the quality and availability of independent factual journalism in Britain.

(3) The digital revolution has this economic impact because, in the age of the search-powered web, the consumer is increasingly unwilling to pay for news, and prefers instead to read selected parts of the news agenda. The web therefore leads to the 'commoditisation' and 'atomisation' of news. Without large audiences, the advertising value of the news is reduced. The internet is capturing a rapidly growing share of total advertising expenditure, but most of this is going into paid search, controlled by new media companies such as Google, which aggregate the news (and other content) but do not create it.

(4) Nonetheless, UK news publishers have turned to the web to extend their reach, increase consumer value and loyalty, and generate at least some revenue, mainly from advertising, to compensate for the revenue lost as a

result of the new commercial and technological pressures. Some have attracted massive but fragmented and transient audiences across the world, at relatively low incremental cost and with minimal marketing. A fundamental challenge is 'monetising' these audiences, whilst also preserving the brand. A further challenge is the enormous popularity of the BBC website, and the very large traffic it attracts. Commercial UK sites believe that its success decreases their traffic, and thus affects advertising revenue—though the extent of this market impact is so far unproven.

(5) In the UK and elsewhere, news publishers are increasingly building digitally mechanised factories, equipped to feed content to a range of media platforms, all day and all week. Newspapers are extending into real-time video, whilst TV broadcasters are expanding their provision of text-based coverage. This process of industry convergence is driven by the remorseless pursuit of productivity and cost-efficiency. Under pressure to exploit content across multiple platforms, many publishers are morphing into a form that favours the processing rather than the generation of content.

(6) The sophisticated and fast-growing public relations industry (financed by wealthy individuals and corporate clients) appears to benefit from this trend. The client-driven, self-promoting incentives of PR align with the cost-cutting incentives of publishers to encourage the rapid absorption of pre-packaged PR material into the twenty-first-century news factories. PR's route to the audience has never been so straightforward. Increasingly, the news that is available to UK citizens is developed by people representing the interests of their clients, rather than those of a diverse media, but this shift is rarely transparent.

(7) In the digital revolution, news publishers are jostling to attract clicks, retain consumer eyeballs, boost advertising revenues and accentuate the visibility of their content in search engines through algorithmic tweaking ('search engine optimisation'). The strategic thinking of publishers is therefore strongly influenced by the 'clickstream' of web consumption—what consumers are looking at and in what quantities. The ascent of click-stream metrics is transformative, resulting in an increasingly crowd-powered news agenda. The independent 'push' of the traditional mass media approach is being splintered by the customised 'pull' of web users, reinforcing the pressure on old media to maximise ratings and readership. By following the ephemeral trails of the global clickstream, publishers are

in danger of morphing into 'digital windsocks'. The professional integrity of journalism could well suffer.

(8) The severity, universality and projected timescale of these trends are debatable, but the ferocity of the current recession is unlikely to provide any respite to news publishers. Therefore, the report concludes that there is a clear danger of a sharp reduction in spending on original newsgathering, including investigative reporting, as well as a further increase in the processing of pre-packaged PR material, a weakening of editorial standards, and a news agenda shaped more and more by the noise of the crowd, perhaps especially for younger citizens.

(9) The report suggests some avenues for redressing the balance and sustaining the economic viability of high-quality news reporting into the twenty-first century. These suggestions address both the commercial and civic side of the equation. On the former, we propose the introduction of targeted tax breaks for public interest news publishing, as well as widening the scope for charitable funding of news-related activities. On the latter, we suggest that there are grounds for radically enhancing the transparency of news publishing—potentially leading to a voluntary form of digital kitemark—not least to improve public trust and appreciation of the civic value of professional journalism.

(10) Any initiatives that are designed to improve the civic profile of journalism should, where possible, favour modes of self-regulation over government interference. It would be dangerous and unpopular to prescribe remedies that are laced with government conditions. At the same time, however, we believe that the government does have a role to play—both in safeguarding the scale of news publishing and in nurturing an informed and participatory digital citizenry, for example through improved access to public data or through the teaching of new forms of digital media literacy.

(11) How the economic viability of news publishing is secured, whilst also enshrining the basic freedom of the Fourth Estate, is clearly a topic for further debate and research. The underlying goal of this report is to draw attention to a structural danger (accentuated by the current recession) for which there may be some practical solutions, and to stimulate debate around the form and implementation of those solutions. It is our hope that the findings in this report will serve as a foundation for follow-on seminars, workshops and other comparative studies.

(12) The report was an independent exercise, carried out under the auspices of the Reuters Institute for the Study of Journalism, based at the University of Oxford. The findings of the report remain the sole responsibility of the author and the wider research team (see below). The views contained herein should not be attributed to the Institute, the University or the various organisations and individuals that we consulted in the course of the research. The funding for the report was kindly made available by the Joseph Rowntree Reform Trust and David Ure, a former executive director of Reuters.

Author and Team Leader: Dr Andrew Currah
Researchers: Harriet Cullinan and Kirsten Westlake
Advisory Group: David Ure, Mandy Cormack, John Lloyd, Geert Linnebank,
Patrick Barwise

Although I (Andrew Currah) have been responsible for writing this report, the underlying research was very much a collaborative effort, developed through conversations with the researchers and the advisory group. The report is therefore written in the first person plural. However, I retain ultimate responsibility for any errors, omissions or statements of fact.

Figures and Tables

1. Introduction

1.1. A digital revolution is transforming news publishing

This report seeks to examine the changing (and challenged) economics of print and television national news publishing in the UK—and in particular, the likely commercial and civic impacts of the changing business of professional journalism. In markets across Europe and North America, news publishers are facing a structural shift in the economic foundations of their industry, as well as a cyclical challenge associated with the global economic slowdown.

The media landscape is becoming more chaotic and fragmented due to the confluence of demographic changes and technological advances. The underlying shift is from *push to pull*; from the generic push of mass media to the customised pull of new media such as blogs, social networks and virtual worlds. Powering this shift is a process we term the *digital revolution*; a revolution in the reach and speed of telecommunications networks; in the processing and storage capabilities of computing; and in the sophistication of software applications, notably on the web.

From a societal perspective, the digital revolution is transforming the character and scale of news consumption. The emerging generation of 'digital natives' exhibits a very different view of media compared to the 'digital immigrants' of older generations. This raises the possibility of a *structural discontinuity* in the news media: in other words, the long-running conversion of younger consumers into reliable consumers of news (for example, as they develop a stake in the future, in the form of family or community) could be disrupted by the emergence of an alternative media ecology, defined by choice and participation, not scarcity and passivity.

For much of the past century, the news was effectively funnelled from professional 'producers' to passive 'consumers', via the scarcity of print and the broadcast spectrum, and typically with some degree of subsidisation from advertising. Barriers to entry remained high, due to the physical costs of gathering the news and obtaining a share of the audience. That economic model is fundamentally challenged by the interactivity of the world wide web, and the plummeting cost of software and computer hardware. As an open network, the web has provided the basis for a radically different media ecology, in which the audience is no longer a passive recipient of the news but rather an active participant in its creation, verification and distribution. Reduced to the simplicity of binary code, the news can now be accessed, shared and combined in ways that were unimaginable just a few years ago.

The digital revolution creates a range of strategic opportunities for news publishers. Aside from the cost of online storage and bandwidth, a website can effectively deliver a wide range of audio, video and text to millions of consumers, at home and abroad, via wired and wireless connections. The result is that news publishers can now assert a virtual presence in foreign markets without any investment in capital-intensive printing facilities or expensive broadcast spectrum. Leading the way, for example, are UK-based newspapers such as the *Daily Mail*, the *Guardian* and *The Times*, which have amassed impressive audiences overseas thanks to the web—notably in the US, where their readership now rivals bastions of American journalism such as the *Los Angeles Times*.

The web also facilitates a new dialogue between producers and consumers of news. Rather than being viewed as a static good, the news is increasingly viewed by the digital consumer as something that is open, social and malleable, which should be probed and extended rather than accepted uncritically. Thus, news publishers are able to supplement their content with the views, thoughts and creative expressions of the 'audience'.

In turn, the web generates a valuable torrent of market and behavioural information: the number and location of digital consumers; the popularity of specific webpages, stories and embedded audio-visual content; the route taken by consumers as they navigate the site; where they spend their time; and so on. Together, these electronic footprints comprise what we term the *clickstream*. The clickstream is significant in strategic and organisational terms because it means that news publishers can now track the performance of their digital assets in real-time; and by implication, closely monitor the productivity and commercial value of their staff.

The digital revolution therefore heralds a new process of mechanisation in news publishing and in particular, the ascent of a new culture of metrics. In the long term, this shift will influence patterns of resource allocation (where publishers choose to invest and disinvest) and professional compensation (by which journalists are rewarded or promoted). As publishers adapt to the pressures of the current economic slowdown, the direction and extent of any cost savings are likely to be shaped by the trails of the clickstream.

Historically, this is interesting. Until now, the market for news has lacked the behavioural metrics that underpin other consumer-driven sectors. The clickstream is arguably as transformative to news publishing as the introduction of 'electronic point of sale' (EPOS) technology in retailing. To be sure, news publishers have always had some degree of consumer feedback; but never before have they had the range, intensity and speed of feedback that the web makes possible.

1.2. The economic foundations of news are weakening

Journalism is produced for sale in the marketplace. The provision of this product (the reporting and analysis of processes and events, from the local to the global scale) relies upon the continued availability of financial capital (to enable the gathering and provision of news). The underlying thesis in this report is that the financial lifeblood of professional journalism is being constrained by the societal and technological dimensions of the digital revolution.

The economics of the news are contingent upon the size and characteristics of the audience, which then determine the value of the news media to advertisers. The problem is that consumers are spending less of their time around traditional channels, such as print and broadcast news, and more of their time around digital channels, which are typically built around the technology of the web (e.g. computers, hand-held devices, third-generation mobile phones, video games consoles).

In turn, that has triggered a reallocation of advertising from traditional to digital platforms; mainly into paid search, but also into classifieds, and more recently display advertising (a vital source of revenues to newspapers and television). The problem for news publishers is that the logic of display advertising (which was suited to the push of mass media) is less effective within the ecology of new media, where consumers prefer instead the convenient pull of targeted search and classified adverts. The latest forecasts indicate that paid search (and Google) will continue to dominate internet advertising for some time.

For advertisers, the unique customisation and reporting capabilities of the web are vastly superior to the static linearity of mass media channels. By mining the clickstream of web consumption, for example, advertisers are able to obtain a highly detailed view of inventory—specifically, the reach of advertising and its return on investment. In a logical but controversial move, websites and advertisers are now turning to the tools of neuroscience to measure the subconscious as well as conscious responses of digital consumers.[1]

The challenge for news publishers, therefore, is how to attract a critical mass of the right audiences around their web content—and crucially, how to do so in a fashion that sustains the interest of advertisers. In theory, news publishers are in a strong position by virtue of their established brands, the reputation of their journalists, and the depth of their archives. On that basis, news publishers have sought to retool and reorganise their newsrooms to take advantage of the web. A vital issue here is the projected value of the digital market versus the actual cost of mobilising for the web.

Quite how news publishers will generate the digital advertising revenues needed to offset the decline of mature channels, and at the same time continue to invest in professional journalism, is still unclear—and a vital issue that this report seeks to address. For a variety of reasons, as we later explain in greater depth, the so-called *monetisation* of web content remains a distant panacea for most news publishers.

First, the social and institutional dynamic of the web is anathema to the pricing strategies of news publishers: their content is effectively *commoditised* into a stream of bits, which is freely available through sharing and linking. As a result, media businesses have had to retreat from subscription-only walled gardens and instead embrace an open access model, supported by advertising (or at the very least, a model premised on the concept of 'first click free').[2]

Second, the hyperlinked structure of the web encourages the *atomisation* of media channels (e.g. newspapers, broadcasts) into distinct shards of information, which tend to be accessed through aggregators and search engines, rather than the home page of a publisher. Our research suggests that over 70 per cent of the traffic to a news website tends to enter from the 'side door' of search results and 'really simple syndication' (RSS) feeds, rather than the home page of the website. Moreover, it is difficult for publishers to keep consumers on their site for longer than a few minutes at a time.

---

[1] This will have long-term implications for the structure and value of online advertising rates. For example, it is logical to assume that websites and technologies with a demonstrable impact on the subconscious behaviour of consumers will ultimately command higher prices in the marketplace.
http://www.mediapost.com/publications/?fa=Articles.showArticleHomePage&art_aid=93319
[2] http://googlewebmastercentral.blogspot.com/2008/10/first-click-free-for-web-search.html

To tackle the challenges of atomised consumption—and hence maximise the commercial value of their web inventory—news publishers are increasingly turning to advertising networks, particularly for support in foreign markets. In doing so, however, publishers are accepting significantly lower advertising rates (sometimes at a discount of 90 per cent). This is due to the deflationary effects of advertising networks. By efficiently matching buyers and sellers of inventory in real-time, the networks are driving down the overall cost of web inventory such as search and display advertising. That trend will be amplified by two related factors: the effects of the economic slowdown; and the glut of inventory created by the convergence of news websites.

Third, the web encapsulates the *paradox of choice*: an abundance of choice has created a scarcity of consumer attention.[3] As Nicholas Carr suggests, the web is moving towards a more *centripetal* structure, in which traffic gravitates around a few sites.[4] This pattern is evident in the UK, where a handful of web domains—operated by Google, Microsoft, Facebook, the BBC and eBay—account for a disproportionate share of internet traffic. In this context, commercial news websites are struggling to capture a critical mass of attention, thereby limiting the growth potential of their advertising revenues.

Fourth, and related, the digital connection between news publishers and the consumer is increasingly mediated by a search engine such as Google. The economics of the web favour skills such as aggregation, indexing and search, as opposed to the original gathering and reporting of the news. Search is now the gatekeeper to the digital consumer. Due to its successful model of paid search, Google dominates internet advertising, and is moving into new domains such as display advertising (e.g. via Double Click and You Tube). With a staff of only 500, Google UK has already secured over 40 per cent of the market for internet advertising and maintains a weekly reach of 30 million users—eclipsing any commercial news website, and just short of the BBC's reach of 40 million.

[3] See B. Schwartz, *The Paradox of Choice: Why More is Less* (Harper Collins, 2004).
[4] http://www.roughtype.com/archives/2008/10/the_centripetal.php

1.3. What's happening to our news

The net result of these trends, we believe, is a digital marketplace that lacks the profitability to sustain existing business models of news publishing. The speed and direction of the digital revolution therefore raise fundamental questions about the future of our news—its quality, its economic underpinning, and its long-term civic function in modern democratic societies. It is our hope that this report will help to shed some light on these questions, and in doing so, outline key areas for commercial and civic debate. The report is structured around three objectives.

The first is to systematically outline the forces that are reshaping news publishing in the UK. We tackle this in Chapters 2–4. The analysis begins by examining the changing profile of the news consumer (in Chapter 2). This leads to a more detailed review of the macro-economic and institutional context in UK news (in Chapter 3). Using this as a backdrop, we then outline (in Chapter 4) the changing sources of news, with specific reference to the rise of the public relations industry, and also the emergence of citizen journalism.

The second objective is to evaluate the response of UK news publishers to the challenges of the digital revolution. Our analysis proceeds in two steps. We begin (in Chapter 5) by describing the strategic thinking that underpins the integration and restructuring of news publishing. This is followed (in Chapter 6) by a more detailed examination of the digital value chain—in particular, how patterns of spending are changing the business and craft of professional journalism.

The third and final objective is to extrapolate from the economic trends a series of possible societal and democratic impacts in the UK. On the premise that the news has a material impact on the decisions and lives of citizens, we present the evidence for a 'democratic deficit' (in Chapter 7). The report concludes (in Chapter 8) by considering some of the possible steps that publishers and government may take to offset the commercial and civic challenges of the twenty-first-century news media.

The report is based upon over 70 interviews with senior participants in the UK news media. In the course of the research, we have consulted a range of academics, consultants, executives, editors, journalists, politicians and regulators. The research sample comprises all of the major publishers, including the BBC, commercial broadcasters and the wide spectrum of newspapers, ranging from the free sheets to paid papers, both tabloid and quality. We have supplemented these data with an eclectic mix of published work from the public and private sectors.

As with any research project, the findings are necessarily illustrative rather than exhaustive. We do not claim to present definitive evidence or comprehensive solutions to the challenges identified. The report lacks the financial data to substantiate the entirety of the economic analysis. This is partly due to the immense secrecy that surrounds the media business, and partly due to the sheer variety of accounting and reporting techniques, which both slow investigation and limit direct comparisons. We have sought to address these limitations by thinking critically, talking widely and developing our analysis incrementally. We are deeply grateful to our interviewees for challenging our assumptions, broadening our field of vision, triangulating points of agreement and jettisoning the inevitable red herring.

The overall story, we believe, is essentially accurate. Nonetheless, the trends identified require further research and comparative study. It is our hope that the material on which this report is based will serve as a stepping-stone to wider debate and inquiry.

2. The news consumer

Journalism works in a marketplace. The success of journalists and their employers is effectively determined by the habits of the news consumer, which have been shaped over time by ongoing societal shifts, as well as disparate technological innovations, from the arrival of television to the broadband internet. Since their inception, newspapers and broadcasters have jostled for the attention of the consumer. In crude terms, their underlying goal is to amass as many 'eyeballs' around the news as possible— and from particular segments of the audience, depending on the editorial voice—using the prevailing technology of distribution and the skill of marketing.

Although desirable, the accumulation of profit is not the only motive at work: it is frequently overshadowed by the raw search for power. The continued survival of many loss-making national papers, such as the *Independent*, is testament to the distinctly non-rational nature of the news media.[5] As Simon Jenkins made clear over 20 years ago, the provision of news is also driven by a variety of non-economic motives, such as the pursuit of status, prestige, philanthropy and political influence, or the fulfilment of public service duties (a statutory requirement in the broadcast arena, but also a stated goal for newspaper publishers such as the *Guardian*).[6]

---

[5] As a result of deepening financial problems, management and shareholders at Independent News & Media (INM) are now debating the sale of the *Independent*, the *Independent on Sunday* and the *Belfast Telegraph*. Denis O'Brien, who holds a 25% stake in INM, views the loss-making titles as a burden on the overall group, which reported a 35.6% slump in operating profits at its UK division in the first half of 2008. The loss-making *Independent* is costing majority owner Tony O'Reilly approximately £10 million per year.

[6] S. Jenkins, *Newspapers: The Power and the Money* (Faber, 1979).

However, the actual gathering, production and dissemination of news is inescapably dependent on some key economic fundamentals—specifically, the size of the audience and its capability to create and sustain revenue over time. In other words: no matter how powerful the philanthropic spirit or the quest for power, the practical costs of journalism demand a robust economic model (which is looking increasingly unstable in the present context). By securing a loyal audience of consumers, news publishers are typically able to generate money in two ways. The first is by selling the content directly and regularly to consumers (for example, in the form of paid newspapers or subscription services). The second is by selling the space around that content to advertisers (for example, in the form of classified or display adverts).

The market for news is geographically variegated due to myriad differences in culture, politics, economics and technology. At an international scale, the news consumer exhibits very different habits in emerging versus mature economies; as demonstrated by the rapid adoption of newspapers in countries such as China or India, versus the decline in print consumption across North America and Western Europe. At a subnational scale, the habits of the news consumer also vary considerably between and within cities and regions. The cultural and political diversity of global cities such as London or Los Angeles poses formidable challenges for metropolitan newspapers and broadcasters, which endeavour to capture the attention and loyalty of the local audience, but generally lack the space, resources and staff to cover the full range of issues affecting residents.

As a mature and highly competitive media market, the UK provides a valuable lens on the changing contours of news consumption. In general, its citizens still rely on television and print for their daily intake of news about the country and the world. UK television news largely depends upon advertising, though Sky News is effectively subsidised by the profits from subscriptions to the BSkyB platform. Newspapers, in contrast, tend to derive approximately 55 per cent of their revenues from advertising, and 45 per cent from circulation sales. In the UK, however, the economic foundations of modern journalism are steadily crumbling due to unprecedented changes in the scale and character of news consumption. The outlook suggests that it will become increasingly difficult for newspapers and broadcasters to assemble large audiences around their content in the foreseeable future.

As the digital revolution gathers pace, a different kind of news consumer is emerging. That consumer has access to a much wider range of news and information sources. Increasingly, consumers expect news media to be free, principally because of the web, but also because of the growing availability of free sheet newspapers in metropolitan markets. The digital revolution empowers the consumer, but also creates problems of choice: as the cacophony of the web intensifies, it is becoming harder for news publishers to secure the attention of the audience, at least in a form that is valuable to advertisers.

To understand the drivers of change, and the challenges facing news publishers, we need to consider the profile and behaviour of the twenty-first-century news consumer. Where are citizens of the UK obtaining their news today? What is the outlook for traditional sources of news? How is the web changing the nature and scale of news consumption? Our research highlights the following points.

2.1. At an aggregate scale, television and newspapers still attract the largest audiences of news consumers in the UK

As Table 2.1 illustrates, television still accounts for the bulk of news consumption across local, regional, UK and world news. Most TV news viewing is still of the established news bulletins on the main channels, notably BBC and ITV, but the launch of 24-hour news channels has increased the dominance of television. As shown in Figure 2.1, audiences of 24-hour news channels such as BBC24 and Sky News have steadily risen over the last decade, with events such as 9/11, the Iraq war or the 7/7 London bombings triggering distinct spikes in viewing. The combined average audiences for these channels increased by over 90 per cent from 57,000 viewers in December 2001 to 94,000 in 2006. After an initial lead, Sky News has recently slipped behind BBC24, which now boasts a larger audience.

Occupying a niche, Channel 4 and Channel 5 News are also performing relatively well. The former regularly attracts a million viewers each night, and viewing levels have remained steady in the past five years despite a 15 per cent reduction in Channel 4's overall audience in that period. Channel 5 News has enjoyed a revival during the past year, thanks to the hiring of Natasha Kaplinsky as its primary news anchor. David Kermode (Editor of Channel 5 News) estimates that viewing in the crucial ABC1 demographic increased by 122 per cent immediately after the arrival of Kaplinsky in the studio. As a whole, the show now attracts around 1.2 million viewers at its 5pm slot versus 400,000 at its 7pm slot.

Source	Local News	Regional News	UK News	World News
TV on main channels	40	56	53	49
TV on digital channels	4	7	14	19
Newspapers	31	17	13	11
Internet	3	2	4	6
Radio	7	8	8	6
Other	4	1	2	2
Not interested/don't know	11	9	6	7
TOTAL	**100%**	**100%**	**100%**	**100%**

Table 2.1. Main sources of news in the UK by category (%)

Source: Adapted from T. Gardam and D. Levy, *The Price of Plurality* (2008), 18.

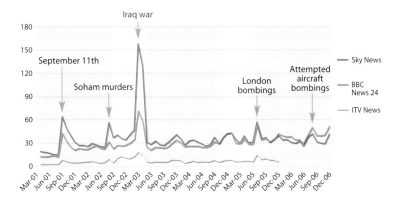

Figure 2.1. Audiences of 24-hour news channels in the UK (000s)

Source: Adapted from Ofcom, *New News, Future News* (2007).

Table 2.1 shows that newspaper consumption is most widespread in the local news category, but loses market share at progressively broader geographical scales (17 per cent of regional news, 13 per cent of UK news, 11 per cent of world news). Between 2002 and 2006, according to researchers at McKinsey, the value of the UK newspaper market expanded by a slim 1.8 per cent, whilst overall circulation declined by 2.8 per cent—a disparity made possible by a 5.2 per cent hike in prices. Relative to other countries, the level of competition between UK national daily newspapers remains extremely intense. The UK has one of the highest levels of newspaper readership in Europe. Despite ongoing declines in circulation, the UK is still seen as one of the world's most dynamic print markets, which continues to attract a significant amount of public relations, branding and marketing activity.

Against this backdrop, it is clear that the internet still accounts for a tiny segment of overall news consumption. In the short term, the web shows no signs of supplanting established modes of news consumption. As many interviewees remarked, there is still a powerful appetite for the edited news programme, on TV and in print, presented alongside a selection of contextually relevant advertising. That makes sense, considering the sheer cacophony of news and information in the multi-channel media environment. But this does not mean that we should understate the long-term significance of the digital revolution, as our following section emphasises.

2.2. Despite their dominant positions, television news viewing and newspaper circulation show signs of a long-term decline in the UK

Over the past decade, audiences for UK television news have steadily fallen. Total annual consumption of national television news (per individual, aged 4+) declined from 103.3 hours in 2001 to 90.8 hours in 2006 (see Table 2.2). The decline has affected all channels, but was sharpest at the commercial providers (for example, -24.9 per cent at ITV1, -11.5 per cent at Channel 4) and weakest at BBC1.

	2006	2005	2004	2003	2002	2001
Total Viewing	90.9	98.1	98.1	108.0	93.6	103.4
BBC1	53.1	53.7	54.0	58.9	50.0	54.1
ITV1	26.3	29.7	29.8	33.1	29.3	35.0
C4	4.6	5.0	4.9	5.4	4.5	5.2
BBC2	3.9	6.5	5.8	6.8	5.8	5.2
Five	3.0	3.2	3.6	3.8	4.0	3.9

Table 2.2. Average viewing of national news on main terrestrial channels (hours, per individual, per annum, aged 4+)

Source: Adapted from Ofcom, *New News, Future News* (2007).

A similar trend can be detected in print consumption. According to the Audit Bureau of Circulation (ABC), there was a universal decline in the circulation of both popular/mid-market (-11 per cent) and quality (-2 per cent) daily newspapers between 1995 and 2005 (see Table 2.3). Looking more closely at the experience of separate titles, however, the picture becomes more complex. Whilst the overall trend points towards declining newspaper consumption, there have been some notable success stories over the past 50 years—for example, the impressive growth rates at *The Sun* (147 per cent), *The Times* (165 per cent) and *The Financial Times* (187 per cent). And despite widespread declines over the past decade, some newspapers have managed to sustain circulation growth—for example, the 41 per cent rise at the *Daily Mail*. The domestic and international success of *The Economist* (which is growing circulation at around 10 per cent per year) is also an important counterpoint to the overall trend of decline.

		1965	1975	1985	1995	2000	2005	Change, 1965–2005	Change, 1995–2005
Popular	*The Sun*	1.32	3.44	4.01	4.05	3.59	3.26	**147%**	-20%
	Daily Mirror	4.99	3.97	3.15	2.42	2.25	1.73	-65%	-29%
	Daily Mail	2.44	1.73	1.82	1.69	1.83	2.38	-3%	**41%**
	Daily Express	3.98	2.82	1.89	1.27	1.05	0.88	-78%	-31%
	Daily Star			1.44	0.74	0.63	0.85		15%
	TOTAL	**12.73**	**11.96**	**12.40**	**10.18**	**9.34**	**9.09**	-29%	-11%
Quality	*Daily Telegraph*	1.34	1.33	1.21	1.06	1.02	0.91	-32%	-14%
	Guardian	0.27	0.32	0.49	0.39	0.39	0.38	**41%**	-3%
	The Times	0.26	0.32	0.48	0.66	0.72	0.69	**165%**	5%
	Independent				0.29	0.23	0.26		-10%
	Financial Times	0.15	0.18	0.23	0.30	0.46	0.43	**187%**	**43%**
	TOTAL	**2.02**	**2.15**	**2.41**	**2.70**	**2.83**	**2.65**	**31%**	-2%

Table 2.3. Detailed breakdown of UK newspaper circulation, 1965–2005 (average net circulation, million copies per day)
Source: Adapted from Audit Bureau of Circulation.

Although it is unlikely to vanish overnight, industry observers agree that the days of mass newspaper distribution are numbered. The recent collapse of print advertising has forced newspaper groups to close a string of local and regional titles. Speaking in November 2008, Carolyn McCall (Chief Executive of the Guardian Media Group) said the 'newspaper is fighting for its survival'.[7] The outlook for tabloids is especially bleak as their core competency (celebrity, soft porn, sports) is increasingly better served on digital media platforms. The executive editor of a prominent tabloid suggested to us that the sector is in a process of 'managed decline'; and that editors are cushioning the immediate impact by reducing cover prices, securing front-page big scoops and expanding promotional giveaways (such as DVDs and digital downloads). Also facing pressure, quality papers

[7] http://www.guardian.co.uk/media/2008/nov/04/bbc-pressandpublishing

are resorting to new revenue streams, such as sponsored editorials and co-branded goods and services—a move that has raised questions about fundamental conflicts of interest in the shaping of the news agenda.[8]

Although beyond the focus of this report, changes in the regional newspaper market are illustrative of the broader economic challenge facing publishers. The decline in print has been especially acute in the regional market, where Enders Analysis forecasts a circulation decline of 12 per cent between 2004 and 2012 (see Table 2.4). That market has been disrupted by the arrival of the 'free sheets', which account for a growing share of circulation.

	Daily	Weekly	Free	Total
2004	1.42	0.41	1.51	3.34
2005	1.35	0.40	1.53	3.28
2006	1.29	0.38	1.56	3.23
2007	1.26	0.36	1.57	3.19
2008	1.19	0.34	1.59	3.12
2009	1.13	0.33	1.60	3.06
2010	1.07	0.32	1.61	3.00
2011	1.03	0.32	1.63	2.98
2012	0.99	0.31	1.64	2.94
Change	**-30%**	**-24%**	**9%**	**-12%**

Table 2.4. Annual circulation of regional newspapers, 2004–2012 (millions)

Source: Adapted from Audit Bureau of Circulation.

Since launching in London in 1999, for example, the *Metro* has become the world's largest free newspaper and the UK's fourth largest newspaper (measured by circulation). According to Kenny Campbell (*Metro*'s Editor-in-Chief), his paper is specifically targeted at 'young, relatively affluent, ambitious, professional and social climbing readers'. As a result, the *Metro* is directly competing with tabloids such as *The Sun*, as well as mid-market papers such as *The Times* and the *Daily Mail*. Newspaper groups are turning to free sheets as a way to attract readers in the sought-after commuter and ABC1 segment, where circulation declines have been sharpest. The spread of the free sheets—coupled to the *free media* attitude of digital news consumers—has put the regional newspaper market under considerable strain, forcing publishers to scale back their operations, adopt

[8] http://mediastandardstrust.blogspot.com/2008/10/how-will-newspapers-make-money-in.html

the free model and/or convert to a cheaper weekly edition.[9] As one senior newspaper executive observed: 'our [freesheet] is now taking 30,000 to 50,000 away from daily sales of our [core product], but clearly you have to be a good cannibal in media these days'.

2.3. The nature and scale of news consumption is shifting to varying degrees in different segments of the market

In the UK, as elsewhere, news consumption is defined by heterogeneity not homogeneity. A recent study by researchers at McKinsey, for example, segmented UK news consumers into eight hypothetical categories, according to demographics, attitudes towards news, the frequency and duration of news consumption, and loyalty to particular brands (see Table 2.5). The study indicates that three categories (sceptical surfers, news lovers and headliners—representing nearly 10 million people) now identify the internet as the most useful way to get their news; and that a further category (citizen enthusiasts—representing 4.4 million people) prioritises the internet over both print and radio news (see Table 2.6).

Although it necessarily simplifies the structure of the market, these data are significant because they suggest that online news already has a strong foothold in a large segment of the market (comprising somewhere between 10 and 14.4 million consumers). The outlook for television and newspapers is further darkened by the steady disengagement of younger consumers from these channels. Market research indicates that these consumers are spending more of their media time on other platforms, such as video gaming and social networking websites.

As Table 2.6 affirms, citizen enthusiasts (the most voracious consumers, according to McKinsey's taxonomy) spend four times longer each day on news consumption than rejecters, typically the youngest consumers. The proliferation of new media platforms is splintering the attention of young consumers, limiting the time they give to the news. The demographic composition of these consumer segments has important implications for the future of news consumption in the UK: for example, the lowest scoring categories in Table 2.6 (i.e. reluctant absorbers, headliners and rejecters) tend to be skewed towards a younger age (see Table 2.7).

The disengagement of younger consumers from news is by no means unique to the present era. For news publishers, consumers tend to become

---

[9] The transition of the *Bath Chronicle* to a weekly publication schedule, for example, delivered a 'significant' increase in margins to its owner (Associated Press), thanks to a rationalised cost-base but relative continuity in the amount of advertising space on sale.

Segment	Characteristics	Size (Million)
Citizen Enthusiasts	Feel a responsibility to know what is happening in the world; news makes them feel connected; consume most news of any segment; go to multiple sources; broad and deep consumption; enjoy the ritual of keeping up with the news, across all platforms	4.4
Sceptical Surfers	Most sceptical about bias and accuracy, relying on multiple sources; like the frequency of update of online news; don't need news to feel connected or intelligent; disengagement from newspapers	2.8
News Lovers	Like citizen enthusiasts, they are heavily engaged in news; rely on TV and online heavily; most trusting segment (don't think sources are biased); reduced breadth of reading, enjoy sources with in-depth analysis; news ritual not important (don't feel a responsibility to read the news)	4.0
Traditional-ists	Enjoy the ritual of reading a newspaper (read more than any other segment); do not feel a responsibility to keep up with the news; do not like online news	3.6
A Few Main Sources	Highly sceptical about bias, so trust a few sources; after TV, most likely to use the radio (not online); do not feel time-pressured; the oldest segment of consumers	3.2
Headliners	Like to skim headlines from a few sources; more interested in facts-only vs deep analysis; find news depressing; time-pressured, and like the efficiency of online sources	3.1
Reluctant Absorbers	Feel the need to keep up with the news but don't enjoy it; reject online sources; prefer to be spoon-fed rather than having to make up their own mind	3.0
Rejecters	Actively reject the news; find it boring/depressing; don't have time, generally uninterested in the news; youngest segment; reject online news sources	2.5

Table 2.5. Profiling the UK news consumer
Source: Adapted from McKinsey, 'An Overview of the News Consumer' (2007): an online survey of 2000 individuals, aged 18 and over, designed to profile news consumers by demographics, attitudes, frequency and duration of news consumption, and brand consumption. It was premised on the assumption that 57% of the UK adult population is online. It was not adjusted for sample bias due to the online nature of the survey

Segment	TV	Print	Radio	Internet	Duration
Citizen Enthusiast	45	17	13	25	88
A Few Main Sources	49	19	25	7	66
News Lovers	36	7	17	40	64
Traditionalists	44	32	13	11	59
Sceptical Surfers	35	8	19	38	58
Reluctant Absorbers	39	24	19	18	52
Headliners	22	10	21	47	31
Rejecters	36	0	29	18	21

Table 2.6. Main sources of news in the UK by consumer segment (%), ranked by average daily duration of total news consumption (minutes)
Source: Adapted from McKinsey, 'An Overview of the News Consumer' (2007).

Segment	18–24	25–34	35–44	45–54	55+
Rejecters	21	7	8	9	7
Reluctant Absorbers	10	14	11	11	8
Headliners	19	12	11	8	10
A Few Main Sources	7	10	11	14	16
Traditionalists	11	10	13	16	23
News Lovers	9	16	19	14	14
Sceptical Surfers	13	12	11	10	6
Citizen Enthusiasts	10	19	16	18	16
TOTAL	**100**	**100**	**100**	**100**	**100**

Table 2.7. Age of news consumers by segment (%)
Source: Adapted from McKinsey, 'An Overview of the News Consumer' (2007).

more interested in their product later in life, typically once their professional and personal life is more established. Many interviewees were optimistic that this pattern will endure. However, the assumption that the current generation of youngsters will automatically evolve into loyal consumers of either newspapers or television, after a certain demographic threshold, is likely to be ill founded.

News publishers may experience a structural discontinuity, as the next generation of consumers become more dependent on digitally interactive media channels, and the demographic-led movement of consumers into print and television begins to ebb. The point is summarised well by Douglas McCabe of Enders Analysis: 'the cycle of young non-readers who start purchasing [news] when their stake in the community emerges (family, home ownership, etc.) is breaking because they are internet natives, not internet immigrants'.

2.4. For the news consumer, the digital revolution creates an abundance of choice but a scarcity of attention

The internet is bringing about a shift from 'push' to 'pull' in the media landscape: that is, existing forms of mass media distribution are being challenged by a raft of new internet-based delivery channels, which facilitate an unparalleled degree of customisation, interactivity and user feedback.

This is not only changing the fundamental nature of media consumption; it also means that consumers can now act as co-producers and co-distributors of content. Propelled by the adoption of broadband—and by the proliferation of websites and online applications—the internet now accounts for 23 per cent of the 'media time' spent by European consumers each year (compared to approximately 31 per cent for TV, 10 per cent for newspapers, 8 per cent for magazines and 28 per cent for radio).[10] Within the younger demographic, the skew is even more pronounced because consumers are devoting significant chunks of their leisure (and working) hours to digital spaces of sociability and fantasy (e.g. Facebook, MySpace or Second Life), as opposed to digital spaces of news and information.

The consumption of online news is limited and fragmented. In their European study, researchers at McKinsey estimated that news accounts for only 2.3 per cent of time spent on online media consumption.[11] This is largely because online news consumption is fleeting in its duration: visitors to the leading UK newspaper websites (as measured by overall traffic) typically only spend a few minutes each day perusing the content. The *Daily Mail* leads the pack, with an average daily visit of only 8.7 minutes; followed by the *Guardian* (5.4 minutes), *News of the World* (3.7 minutes), *The Sun* (3.7 minutes) and *The Times* (3.3 minutes).[12] In contrast, McKinsey estimates that, on average, consumers spend roughly *eight times* longer reading a physical newspaper, compared to the equivalent time they spend at a newspaper website.[13]

These data suggest that consumers tend to be more directed in their navigation and use of online news, in contrast to the casual browsing that characterises newspaper consumption. The short duration of online news consumption means it is even harder for news publishers to monetise their content. Advertisers are increasingly demanding access to clearly defined and engaged audiences, not transitory eyeballs. However, as digital information becomes more abundant, consumer attention is becoming scarcer.

Reflecting the paradox of choice that is common to other markets, the consumption of web content is becoming narrower even as choice widens.[14] In economic terms, the 'non-rivalrous' nature of digital information—that is, quick publication, rapid distribution and simultaneous consumption—reinforces this asymmetric pattern of attention. Overwhelmed by the choice of the web, consumers tend to flock to just a handful of websites. In a recent paper for Information Research, for example, Chun-Yao Huang and colleagues concluded that 'the more page-views a Web user makes,

---

[10] McKinsey, *Reshaping Publishers for Digital* (McKinsey, 2008). Based on surveys in UK, France, Germany, Italy and Spain.
[11] It is virtually impossible to know with any precision exactly how much news consumers are exposed to whilst surfing, given the diversity of information sources and the multiple channels through which news can flow.
[12] Adapted from McKinsey, *Reshaping Publishers for Digital*. Calculated in Feb. 2008.
[13] ibid.
[14] For a wider discussion, see Schwartz, *The Paradox of Choice*.

the higher the proportion of page-views concentrated on a relatively small set of anchoring or core websites'.[15] Such a pattern is reflected in the latest web analytics. According to research by Hitwise.com, UK internet users currently spend over 32 per cent of their time at only 20 websites. Table 2.8 shows that a search engine (Google.co.uk), a social network (Facebook.com), a portal (Microsoft Live.com) and a shopping site (eBay.co.uk) represent the UK's most popular websites, when ranked by share of overall internet traffic. Delving further, we can see that just 10 domains operate those 20 websites: Google accounts for a disproportionate share of traffic (13.17%), followed by Microsoft (5.77%), Facebook (3.16%), the BBC (2.49%) and eBay (2.4%).

Rank	Website	Share
1	www.google.co.uk	8.22
2	www.facebook.com	3.16
3	Mail.live.com	3.00
4	www.ebay.co.uk	2.40
5	www.google.com	1.83
6	uk.msn.com	1.75
7	www.youtube.com	1.41
8	www.bebo.com	1.24
9	uk.yahoo.com	1.10
10	news.bbc.co.uk	1.08
11	www.microsoft.com	1.02
12	www.bbc.co.uk	0.94
13	uk.mail.yahoo.com	0.84
14	www.wikipedia.org	0.70
15	www.myspace.com	0.66
16	news.bbc.co.uk/sport	0.65
17	www.orange.co.uk	0.63
18	images.google.co.uk	0.60
19	www.gmail.com	0.58
20	uk.youtube.com	0.53

Table 2.8. Top 20 UK websites (ranked by % of internet traffic)

Source: Adapted from http://www.hitwise.co.uk

The complete absence of any commercial news websites in Table 2.8 underscores the profound challenges facing news publishers as they seek to attract and retain the attention of consumers on the web. The picture

---

[15] http://informationr.net/ir/12-4/paper324.html

becomes even clearer if we consider the search habits of the contemporary digital consumer: according to Hitwise, UK consumers tend to search (predominantly via Google) for terms such as Facebook, Bebo, eBay and You Tube (see Table 2.9). Based on this evidence, therefore, it is apparent that, for most consumers, the web is a place of sociability, shopping, leisure and fantasy. When it does occur, online news consumption tends to be fleeting, scattered and largely depends on the BBC's extensive web domain (see next chapter).

Rank	Search Term	Share (%)
1	facebook	1.39
2	Bebo	1.18
3	Ebay	1.06
4	youtube	0.88
5	you tube	0.40
6	myspace	0.29
7	argos	0.28
8	bbc	0.22
9	amazon	0.19
10	bbc weather	0.18

Table 2.9. Top internet search terms in the UK (May 2008)

Source: Adapted from http://www.hitwise.co.uk

2.5. Search engines and aggregators are now the principal gateway to the digital news consumer, thus wresting control from publishers

The limited extent and duration of online news consumption must be understood within the context of two key trends. First, the internet is having a commoditisation effect on the supply of news: consumers now have free access to the latest news across a network of aggregators, search engines, blogs and 'really simple syndication' (RSS) feeds, located outside the bastions of professional journalism. The web 2.0 bazaar offers consumers a bewildering choice of information sources, many of which are attracting loyal audiences, especially within specialist areas, as well as breaking stories before established news publishers.

The web has cemented the view that online news should be free, thereby engendering a strong reluctance to pay (either through micro-payments or subscriptions for news feeds). Consequently, publishers have had to retreat from 'fire-walled' subscription news services and instead embrace the ethos of permanent and open access, not least to enhance their visibility in search engines.[16]

Second, the internet is having an atomisation effect on the consumption of news: the hyperlinked structure of the internet has dismantled broadcast news and print editions into individual stories, which are found and read à la carte, typically with the help of an aggregator or search engine. Aggregators continue to abound; services such as Blog Lines or Google Reader funnel a customised selection of stories direct to consumers within a single webpage. Meanwhile, search continues to be monopolised by Google, which as Table 2.10 makes clear, now accounts for almost 90 per cent of internet searches in the UK. Between 2007 and 2008, competitors such as Microsoft and Yahoo! all suffered declines in market share.

Engine	May 2007	May 2008	Change
Google	78.3	87.3	9.0
Yahoo!	8.6	4.1	-4.5
MSN	5.5	3.7	-1.8
Ask	5.0	3.1	-1.9

Table 2.10. Distribution of internet searches in the UK by platform (%)
Source: Adapted from Hitwise UK; note that market shares combine searches from .co.uk and .com domains.

Nonetheless, the search market remains technologically dynamic as competitors and innovators explore different ways of displacing Google, which for the large part has relied upon external acquisitions (as opposed to internal innovation) to expand its range of services and applications.

Google's algorithmic model faces potentially disruptive competition from new search engine technology—such as Mahalo (a human-edited approach to search), Silo Breaker (a semantic model) or Wikia (an open source project). Whether and to what extent those search engines will eat into Google's market share is still unclear. What is important to note is that the technologies for aggregating, navigating and packaging online news are constantly becoming more sophisticated and consumer-friendly—though they are still vulnerable to algorithmic failure (see Chapter 8). The evolution of search technology is a vital part of the jigsaw, as search engines increasingly mediate the connection between consumers and online news.

---

[16] The exception to this trend is specialist or premium information sources (e.g. financial news, strategic analyses); but even here, the rising tide of commoditised content has the capacity to erode established business models.

For example, our research suggests that over 70 per cent of the traffic to the leading UK newspaper websites originates from an external hyperlink; search results are believed to be the dominant generator of that traffic, followed by RSS feeds. The picture is different for a portal such as the BBC, which has the reputation and breadth of content to attract users directly (see also Table 2.8 above). As we describe in Chapter 3, the BBC has an unrivalled digital portfolio comprising over 200 individual websites, which attracts 3.6 billion page impressions each month from users worldwide.

Increasingly, however, an aggregation or search tool is seen as the logical place for news consumption to begin—not least because of their user-friendly graphical interface, the classification of stories, and the ability to compare headlines from multiple news outlets worldwide (see Figure 2.2). The sheer variety of news content on the web is likely to boost the appeal of reliable, trusted and comprehensive aggregators of headlines from around the world. That poses challenges for news publishers, which must now invest in the systems and training necessary to enhance the exposure of their stories in search engines and retain the attention of consumers once they enter the site (see Chapter 6).

Figure 2.2. Packaging the web of news: screen shot of Google News
Source: http://news.google.com/

Search is now the gateway to the online news consumer. That shift is a key concern to news publishers, which view the rise of aggregators such as Google News as a potential threat to high-quality, plural news provision. Speaking to the House of Lords Select Committee on Communications, the Chairman of Guardian Media Group, Paul Myners, explained that, although online aggregators deliver valuable traffic to their web properties, especially from abroad, they also extract revenue 'directly from news content without investing in journalism'.[17] Although Google does not generate revenue directly from the aggregation of news (due to the absence of advertising around stories), its News product contributes to the appeal and 'stickiness' of the Google brand as a whole. In effect, Google uses search to 'free ride' on the newsgathering of broadcasters, newspapers and wire agencies. We discuss the evolving relationship between Google and news publishers in greater detail in Chapter 5.

The key point is that the economics of the web increasingly favour aggregators and search engines, as opposed to established producers of journalism. With a staff of only 500, for example, Google UK enjoys operating margins of over 30 per cent on revenues of £1.3 billion. Its UK reach, meanwhile, is estimated to be 30 million; just short of BBC TV's approximately 40 million, and vastly greater than any other news publisher, either online or in print and broadcast.[18]

Together, these broad changes—commoditisation plus atomisation— are simultaneously eroding the integrity and commercial value of packaged news products, and thereby empowering news consumers with greater choice. Of all the consumer segments, for example, citizen enthusiasts are believed to visit over 17 news brands per week; 7 on the internet alone, compared to 4.6 on television, 3.3 in print and 1.8 on radio (see Table 2.11). Sceptical surfers and news lovers are also exposed to more brands on the web than in print or on television.

Segment	Television	Newspapers	Magazines	Radio	Websites
Citizen Enthusiasts	4.6	3.3	0.9	1.8	7.0
Sceptical Surfers	3.7	1.1	0.5	1.5	4.9
News Lovers	3.7	1.3	0.2	1.4	4.1
Traditionalists	3.8	3.0	0.4	1.5	3.0
Overall UK	3.5	1.9	0.5	1.4	3.6

Table 2.11. Weekly exposure to news brands by consumer segment
Source: Adapted from McKinsey, 'An Overview of the News Consumer' (2007).

This is significant, because it indicates that news consumers are likely to acquire information from a much wider range of sources online. It also highlights the potential efficiencies of online news consumption.

---

[17] House of Lords Select Committee on Communications, *The Ownership of the News*, vol. 1, *Report*, (Stationery Office), p. 14.
[18] Adapted from data submitted to the House of Lords Select Committee by Guardian Media Group, Sept. 2007.

Despite its fleeting nature, it is plausible to assume that search tools, combined with customised feeds and navigational web histories (e.g. Digg, Delicious), are enhancing the availability and utility of news to consumers—such that many individuals are likely to be receiving, on aggregate, more relevant information than before the age of the web. The internet also simplifies the delivery and display of relevant contextual information, such as a story's back-history, related coverage or reader comments and reviews—value-added content that the publishers are now seeking to deploy on their websites (see Chapter 6). Whether these developments are actually broadening consumers' horizons, or instead spawning customised *echo chambers*, is a topic for later discussion—not least because the internet can also deconstruct and detach information from its context (see Chapters 7 and 8).

For the time being, it is sufficient to note that the interactivity of the web is beginning to transform news consumption, and that to succeed news publishers must create websites that engage the interest and attention of audiences. Achieving that degree of stickiness is proving difficult, as the next chapter explains. To date, news publishers have struggled to find ways of monetising online news consumption.

3. The economics of news

Changes in the nature and scale of UK news consumption are eroding and redefining the economic foundations of professional journalism. News publishers are facing a long-term decline in their core revenue streams, and as a result are struggling to cover the underlying costs of original journalism. To survive, they will need to build successful web properties that can capture a share of internet advertising, sufficient to generate revenues able to pay for original reporting and informed editing.

In the quest for digital success, news publishers are increasingly looking overseas for new audiences; but how or whether those audiences can be valued and monetised through advertising is still extremely unclear, not least because of the global economic slowdown. Despite attracting a wealth of international traffic, news websites are struggling to climb out of the poverty of a digital presence; operating and marketing costs still outweigh revenues by a long margin.

The search for digital monetisation is accentuating the strategic importance of web statistics. In an effort to better understand the characteristics of audiences, and thereby provide more detailed measurement capabilities to relevant advertisers, news publishers are increasingly relying on the *clickstream* of online news consumption: that is, the electronic footprints that are left behind as consumers navigate, access and share web content. In this way, publishers can better target content and advertising.

The digital evolution of commercial news brands must also be understood in relation to the competitive dynamics of the UK media landscape; in particular, the public funding and digital ambitions of the BBC, which has unparalleled resources at its disposal to develop and extend its online news offering. Whilst the BBC has built a successful website, there is no evidence that its presence significantly impacts the vitality of commercial rivals—though as this report was being finalised, the BBC Trust vetoed management plans to create 60 new video sites to provide local news for the BBC website at a cost of £68m, in part because the Trust judged that it would adversely affect the position of local newspapers. We will consider the concerns of the commercial sector alongside the public value of the BBC.

Together, these inter-related issues provide the backdrop to the changing economic foundations of UK news publishing. We address each in turn.

3.1. News publishers face long-term declines in their core businesses, as advertising spend migrates to digital platforms

It is becoming increasingly difficult for television broadcasters and newspapers to assemble audiences that have the scale and demographic characteristics necessary to sustain the interest and investment of advertisers. As consumers spend a growing proportion of their media time on the internet, advertisers are starting to reallocate their creative energies and investment from mass media channels to the new media of the web, which promises more interactive, customised and performance-driven forms of consumer engagement.[19]

Researchers at McKinsey estimate, for example, that over 50 per cent of the forecast growth in global internet advertising will derive from the direct reallocation of advertising spend. The evolving composition of UK advertising spend, by media channel, is portrayed in Table 3.1, which highlights the rapid growth of internet advertising and in contrast, the shrinking market share of both television and print.

In 2007, internet advertising represented over 15 per cent of total advertising spend in the UK, compared to a share of 7 per cent globally.[20] The Internet Advertising Bureau confirms that the UK is allocating a larger share of advertising spend to the internet than other countries, even the US.[21] For the UK media, the net result of this shift is likely to be a bigger advertising pie, depending on the severity and length of the recession.

---

[19] That has not stopped news publishers experimenting with new ways of generating advertising from their core channels. In the US, for example, several affiliates of Fox News have begun to use product placements in broadcasts as an additional revenue stream:
http://www.guardian.co.uk/world/2008/jul/23/usa.mcdonalds
[20] See the forecast by Zenith Optimedia in 2006:
http://www.zenithoptimedia.com/gff/pdf/Adspend%20forecasts%20December%202006.pdf
[21] http://www.iabuk.net/en/1/iabadspend2006.mxs

The disruption to news publishers has been most acute in classified advertising, which has long been essential to the economic health of newspapers, in the regional market especially. On the internet, classified advertising is able to connect buyers and sellers more efficiently, generally for free. The market outlook is captured in Table 3.2, which contrasts the rise of the online classifieds (forecast to rise to 33 per cent of spend by 2011, up from 2 per cent in 2002) with the catastrophic decline of regional classifieds (forecast to drop to 44 per cent of spend in 2011, down from 62 per cent in 2002).[22]

	2002	2004	2006	2008 (forecast)
TV	31	30	28	27
Newspapers	40	38	34	30
Internet	2	6	14	20
Magazines	16	14	13	12
Other	11	12	11	11

Table 3.1. Distribution of UK advertising spend by media, 2002–2008 (%)
Source: Adapted from Price Waterhouse Coopers, *Global Entertainment and Media Outlook* (2008). 'Other' includes radio, outdoor and direct mail marketing

	2002	2005	2008 (forecast)	2011 (forecast)
Regional newspapers	62	61	55	44
National newspapers	15	13	12	9
Consumer magazines	5	5	5	4
Business & professional publications	15	13	12	10
Internet	2	8	17	33

Table 3.2. UK classified advertising revenues by channel
Source: Adapted from McKinsey, Reshaping Publishers for Digital (2008).

UK media groups largely failed to foresee the disruptive impact of the internet; and are now seeking to reaggregate control over classified advertising, through the creation of interlinked web properties (spanning cities and specific sectors, such as recruitment and motors). Many publishers, for example, are now seeking to diversify their digital revenue streams by forging revenue-sharing partnerships with e-commerce websites, such as travel or dating.

[22] The overall classified advertising market is forecast to grow to £3.38 billion by 2011, up from £3.11 billion in 2002.

3.2. To effectively monetise their web content, news publishers will need to harness the capabilities of internet advertising formats

The future of news publishers will be shaped to a significant degree by their ability to understand and harness the interactive features of internet advertising, across the search, display and classified formats. Paid search is still the most popular format among advertisers by a long margin, and is likely to weather the economic slowdown (as the impressive earnings of Google continue to demonstrate).[23] As we describe in Chapter 6, news publishers are cultivating new skills—related to areas such as *search engine optimisation* and *semantic enrichment*—to enhance the visibility of their content on the web.

However, access to these new formats—notably, search and display—is increasingly mediated by advertising networks, which are using economies of scale to drive down the price of online advertising inventory. Take display ads: the 'cost per thousand impressions' can be 90 per cent lower through a network, compared to the equivalent cost of a direct deal with a news publisher. That differential is leading some publishers to devise their own advertising sales infrastructure, or to find ways of increasing the scarcity (and hence the value) of desirable inventory. But in the race for digital success, publishers have effectively created a glut of inventory that is proving difficult to sell. For that reason, the majority of publishers view networks as the most efficient way of monetising web inventory; they are settling for some revenue, albeit at a lower price, rather than leaving inventory unsold.

By conveniently aggregating publishers and advertisers, advertising networks are able to match supply and demand more efficiently; thereby facilitating the rapid allocation of advertising inventory around web content. This is particularly crucial during unexpected traffic spikes, when publishers need to quickly allocate inventory around new content. The digital surge created by the financial crisis in September 2008, for example, was supposedly a boon to publishers; but many were left with unsold inventory, due to the absence of established advertising deals.[24]

A recent study (commissioned by the Interactive Advertising Bureau and Bain & Co.) found that media companies are increasingly turning to advertising networks to sell excess inventory, notably on newspaper sites.[25]

---

[23] http://www.nytimes.com/2008/10/17/technology/companies/17google.html
[24] http://www.nytimes.com/2008/10/13/business/media/13adco.html
[25] http://www.iab.net/digital_pricing_research

The estimated proportion of inventory sold through networks increased from 5 per cent in 2006 to 30 per cent in 2007. In parallel, publishers with access to an advertising network have reported declines in the proportion of inventory that remains unsold. Looking ahead, publishers are likely to rely even more on advertising networks as they seek to monetise their expanding digital platforms. This includes Google, which is expanding into display ads (via its Double Click acquisition), and also extending its auction model to print and broadcast.

The market for internet advertising is being fuelled by a number of factors. Crucially, there is still a disparity between the allocation of media time (i.e. the platforms where consumers spend their time) and the allocation of media spend (i.e. the platforms where advertisers spend their money). According to McKinsey, newspapers and magazines have relatively inflated ratios (3:3 and 2:1 respectively); whilst the internet has a ratio of media spend to media time of only 0:8, indicating potential for growth. In other words, consumer use of the web justifies a higher level of advertising spend.

The internet is more appealing to advertisers than broadcast channels such as television or radio because, like print, it has lower creative production costs and advertising campaigns tend to have shorter lead times. Moreover, the internet provides advertisers with unique customisation capabilities, including the tracking and adaptation of advertising messages to the behaviour of individual consumers. Indeed, advertisers are becoming far more stringent in their demands of internet advertising; for example, many now expect websites to meet rigorous performance standards, in an effort to extract a clearer return on their web investment (see below).

But the internet is not a homogeneous medium. According to Adam Smith, Futures Director at WPP-owned media agency Group M, the 'growth rate of internet advertising is actually a blend of three distinct businesses growing at different speeds: search, display and classified'.[26] All of which are significant to the commercial future of news publishers.

The UK market for internet advertising can be broken down as follows.[27] In 2007, the bulk of spending was directed towards search-related advertising (£1.62 billion), which remains a heavily concentrated market, dominated by Google. This was supplemented with an additional spending of £592 million on display advertising and £585 million on classified advertising. By 2010, the UK market for internet advertising is projected to reach £4.36 billion; with £2.45 billion deriving from search, £1 billion from display and

---

[26] http://www.guardian.co.uk/media/2008/may/19/digitalmedia.advertising
[27] Adapted from Internet Advertising Bureau, WARC and Zenith Optimedia.

£876 million from classifieds. As consumer adoption continues, internet advertising will steadily eclipse established channels such as print and television. Next year, for example, UK advertisers are expected to spend more online (an estimated £3.6 billion) than on television adverts (£3.4 billion).

At the heart of this transition is a growing belief in the capabilities of the internet as a platform for display advertising. As Sebastian Grigg (former Head of Media Investment Banking, Deutsche Bank, now at Credit Suisse) told us, 'the web is eating into television advertising to an extent not foreseen just a few years ago'.

That change has been brought about by the increased sophistication of display technologies, which were formerly confined to features such as banner ads and interactive buttons. In particular, advertisers are now beginning to allocate more of their investment to building online brand awareness—notably, through new technologies such as rich media and flash video, which offer new opportunities for audience engagement. That spend is crucial, as consumers are increasingly using brands to search and navigate the internet: Hitwise estimates, for example, that 88 per cent of UK internet searches are for branded search terms.[28]

In fact, a greater proportion of brand spend is likely to migrate to the internet as it becomes progressively harder to assemble large, predictable audiences around mature channels due to the fragmentation of news and media consumption. To be sure, the internet is far from proven as a platform to launch and sustain brand building; but its unique customisation, monitoring and reporting characteristics make it an ideal candidate for experimentation with display advertising.

As a result, the value of online display inventory (especially around premium content) is being driven higher in places. That trend lies behind ITV's stated goal to increase digital revenues from its website to £150 million by 2010 (up from £30 million in 2007).[29] Advertisers are increasingly turning to new display formats, combined with behavioural targeting and multi-platform integration, to reach online audiences. By meeting these expectations, news publishers could conceivably boost profits from their digital platforms.

So, the long-term outlook for the internet advertising market is over-whelmingly positive. UK news publishers are in a strong position to capture a share of that market, particularly in the display arena. Recent surveys by the Newspaper Marketing Agency suggest that newspaper advertising continues to play a powerful role in raising brand awareness among

[28] http://www.hitwise.co.uk/press-center/hitwiseHS2004/brands.php
[29] http://www.paidcontent.co.uk/entry/
419-itv-aims-for-150-million-online-revenue-emphasis-on-display-and-targete/

consumers, especially when combined with a TV campaign. For newspapers, the web is particularly enticing because it provides access to the audio-visual budgets of media buying groups, a market that previously lay beyond their reach.

To date, however, both print and broadcast news publishers have struggled to monetise their web properties. The economic slowdown has further dampened the outlook. As a result, digital revenues are not increasing fast enough to offset the decline of their mature business channels. In fact, Enders Analysis estimates that key growth sectors for news publishers, such as online display advertising, flattened out during 2008.

3.3. As the digital revolution gathers pace, news publishers are struggling to generate significant revenues from their web properties

The internet enables content owners to package and sell their content direct to audiences, either through micro-payments (e.g. to purchase individual items) or subscription services (e.g. to gain access to a given database). With the exception of specialist information (e.g. business, intelligence or investment), these models have failed to gain traction in the area of online news due to the prevailing 'free media' attitude among consumers.

As such, news publishers have been forced, to varying degrees, to retreat from the walled garden model and instead embrace an open access model of web distribution that generates revenue through advertising. Even premium publications such as the *Financial Times* and *The Economist*—former stalwarts of the walled garden approach—have loosened the restrictions on their website to enable periods of unlimited access.

In an effort to buttress their open access model, media groups have spent heavily on digital acquisitions—for example, websites that are anchored around specific cities, regions and markets (motoring, property, recruitment, travel). In one of the largest deals, Guardian Media Group spent £1.14 billion acquiring Trader Media. Daily Mail & General Trust (DMGT), meanwhile, now oversees one of the largest web empires, comprising nearly 140 websites. In total, the top five newspaper groups have invested close to £1.6 billion in digital media since 2001: selected acquisitions by DMGT and Trinity Mirror are depicted in Table 3.3.

Newspaper Group	Year	Acquisition	Price Paid
DMGT	2001	Loot	45.0
	2004	Find a Property	13.8
		Job Site	36.0
	2005	Top Consultant	4.1
		Office Recruit	
	2006	Prime Location	48.0
		Villa Renters	3.0
		Production Base	17.0
		Retail Careers	
		Auto Exposure	22.0
		Simply Switch	
		Girls Date for Free	46.5
		Dating for Parents	
		Loopy Love	
		Pocado	
	2007	Jobs Group	10.0
	2008	Oil Careers	n/a
Trinity Mirror	2005	Hot Group	50.5
		Secs in the City	3.5
		Gaap Web	13.0
		Smart New Homes	16.6
	2006	Hot Group Consultancy	11.2
		Email 4 Property	4.4
	2007	Totally Legal	11.8
		Totally Financial	
		Homes Overseas	5.9
		Show House	
		What House	
	2008	Career Engineer	2.3

Table 3.3. Selected digital acquisitions by DMGT and Trinity Mirror since 2001 (£million)
Source: Adapted from Enders Analysis (2008).

The underlying goal behind these acquisitions, as a senior newspaper executive told us, is to create an interlinked empire of web properties. Publishers might then be able 'to aggregate a critical mass of eyeballs around the brand' and therefore 'reassert leadership in the online advertising market' (notably, across classifieds and display).

Newspaper groups are still some way from realising that goal. Digital revenues from web properties remain limited. To some extent, as the executive went on to explain, 'the rescue of the online classified business remains separate from the digital rescue of news'. Whilst the former would help to subsidise the latter, it is not immediately clear how the two would be combined online. In other words, an integrated package of 'news plus embedded classifieds' is somewhat anachronistic in a digital form.

For the time being, moreover, the rescue of news is complicated by the fragmented and fleeting nature of online news consumption which means that publishers still lack the critical mass of eyeballs necessary to monetise their digital platforms. There is a stark disparity, for example, between the online and offline audiences of leading UK newspapers, as depicted in Table 3.4. The challenge is compounded by the wide gulf between revenues per user online versus offline: McKinsey estimates that online revenues per user for newspapers and magazine groups are, at best, only one-twentieth of equivalent offline revenues per user (due to the collective value of advertising and circulation, albeit declining).

	UK Online Audience (Unique Users)	UK Offline Audience (Sales)
Daily Mail	0.18	2.16
Guardian	0.23	0.33
News of the World	0.38	3.06
The Sun	0.29	3.07
The Times	0.13	0.61

Table 3.4. Daily reach of UK newspapers (millions)
Source: Adapted from McKinsey, *Reshaping Publishers for Digital* (2008). Online audiences calculated in Feb. 2008; offline audiences in Jan. 2008.

3.4. The web is redefining the geographical reach of media brands, sparking competition among news publishers for foreign audiences

As news publishers try to build successful web properties, a tectonic shift is underway in the economic foundations of the sector. That shift is redefining the very nature of news brands, as the web exposes publishers from print and broadcast to a vast audience of consumers worldwide. For example, the *Guardian* now has a larger readership in the US than the *Los Angeles Times*. Meanwhile, the BBC has used the web to bolster its position as one of the world's most trusted news sources: bbc.co.uk now receives over 3.6 billion page impressions each month from users worldwide.

In the age of the web, news brands are no longer confined to the shores of the UK. Rather, they have the capacity to function as digital hubs around which dispersed clusters of news consumers can gather. The web also enables news brands to aggregate readers around a particular lens on the world.[30]

The *Daily Mail* and *Guardian*, for example, have attracted significant audiences from the US—without any investment in marketing—thanks to the defining features of their respective editorial voices. The former attracts viewers with its populist, right-wing style, whilst the latter positions itself as the world's leading liberal voice. The editorial orientation of news brands on the web can in fact serve as a catalyst for the mobilisation and aggregation of particular political and ideological viewpoints. In fact, it is arguable that the web makes it even more essential for news publishers to have a clear editorial voice.

The geographical reach of web-based news brands is reason for celebration. As we discuss in Chapter 5, news publishers are betting that globalization through digitally integrated platforms will eventually be the saviour of journalism, as audiences and advertising around traditional platforms dwindle.

Despite their international success, however, news publishers have struggled to convert foreign audiences—no matter how large—into significant advertising revenues. That is largely because of the difficulties inherent to the analysis and valuation of such audiences: who are the readers, and what products or services might they be interested in? Non-UK web traffic is less attractive to core UK advertisers. To effectively sell advertising inventory around their international content, UK news publishers now realise that they need to better understand their foreign audiences and therefore forge partnerships with media buyers and advertising networks.

For example, both the *Independent* and *Daily Telegraph* are now using AdGent 007 to place adverts around content that will be viewed by foreign audiences. Through local relationships with media buyers, AdGent claims to improve advertising rates for UK publishers by 10–20 per cent (though, as noted above, advertising networks can also exert a deflationary pressure on rates).[31] Meanwhile, the *Guardian* is using Reuters to sell inventory on its US site, and Ad2One to sell inventory in the Singaporean, Australian and Irish markets. Taking a different tack, Times Online relies on the advertising sales team at the *Wall Street Journal* to sell its US inventory.[32]

---

[30] For a discussion of related issues, see L. Clausen, 'Localising the Global: Domestication Processes in International News Production', *Media, Culture and Society*, 26/1 (2004): 25–44.

[31] http://www.ft.com/cms/s/0/24d49cf2-9dff-11dd-bdde-000077b07658.html?nclick_check=1

[32] http://www.paidcontent.co.uk/entry/419-independentcouk-latest-to-sell-ads-to-foreign-eyeballs/

3.5. The digital clickstream is reshaping the content strategy of news publishers, albeit in an incremental and covert fashion

> *News organisations are now driven by ratings figures and a story's potential to generate revenue through advertising—they now want news about celebrities, starlets, gossip, violence, large brands and snappy sound bites and statistics … News organisations are increasingly driven by the commercial potential of a story.*
> (Lucy Hadfield, Managing Partner, Crucible Partners)

The challenges of digital monetization have accentuated the strategic importance of the clickstream to news publishers. Thanks to the interactivity of the web, news publishers and journalists are able to track, in real-time, which stories, videos and podcasts are most popular amongst the audience.

That is a revolutionary change in the nature of journalism—analogous perhaps to the transformative impact of 'electronic point of sale' (EPOS) data to supply chain management and marketing in the retail industry. To be sure, journalists have always had some degree of feedback from readers: the size of the audience and whether it is growing or shrinking is the important, if crude, factor, supplemented by the letters pages as well as qualitative analytical techniques such as consumer surveys and focus groups. And publishers have always sought to tailor their content to the views and habits of their respective audience. But never before have journalists or publishers had the range, intensity and speed of audience feedback that the web makes possible.

A tour at any of the multimedia newsrooms around London will quickly reveal the new fascination with the tastes and habits of the digital news consumer. Towering over the *Daily Telegraph*'s flagship newsroom, for example, is a giant screen that displays, in a provocative league table format, the most popular stories on the newspaper's website (see Figure 3.1).

Our research indicates that data from the clickstream is beginning to impact the operation of newsrooms. In several interviews, editors confirmed that data from the web is now regularly consulted throughout the day. To varying degrees, depending on the publisher, the clickstream shapes the allocation of resources between stories, particularly if editors identify a surprisingly popular or breaking story that can attract the traffic (and advertising) to justify the allocation of additional resources.

It is difficult to quantify the actual impact of the clickstream on coverage; but suffice to say there is a growing tension between editorial values and knowledge of what will actually generate revenue. The impact on journalists is also significant. Analysis of the clickstream, cross-referenced with data about advertising inventory, means that editors can monitor the exact contribution of stories to the bottom line. In that context, journalists will be under greater pressure in the future to perform according to new web metrics.

Figure 3.1. The *Daily Telegraph* newsroom, Victoria, London
Source: *Reproduced with permission of Telegraph Media Group.*

Quite where the clickstream will ultimately lead news publishers and news brands is subject to fierce debate. Some argue it will distort journalism by ushering editorial attention away from public-interest stories towards more populist, click-friendly topics. In contrast, others see it as a positive force, which will encourage news publishers to pay closer attention to the views of their audience, thereby improving the quality of the product. We consider the implications of the clickstream for news publishers and journalists in more detail in Chapters 5 and 6.

At this point, it is sufficient to note that a new culture of web metrics and performance targets is beginning to take root in multimedia newsrooms, albeit in an incremental and largely covert fashion. By analysing the clickstream, news publishers are hoping to better understand the digital news consumer, and so build successful web properties.

In large part, news publishers are following the clickstream to satisfy advertisers, who are demanding rigorous and transparent forms of online inventory allocation, to enable more accurate calculations of return on investment. In fact, the detailed nature of the clickstream is engendering new metrics of value among advertisers: for example, the degree and quality of engagement with the consumer, as opposed to pure click-through rates or time spent viewing a message. This new approach is being cemented by the rise of more sophisticated, multi-platform advertising campaigns, which harness the distributed capabilities of web 2.0 applications (e.g. sponsorships, contests, micro-sites, communities) to connect with the audiences.

The clickstream dovetails with the new demands of advertisers, by facilitating what is known as *behavioural targeting*: advertising inventory that is dynamically shaped and priced according to its exposure to the habits of specific consumer segments. The good news for publishers is that such techniques have the capacity to boost the rates they can charge advertisers. For example, the *Financial Times* now offers behavioural advertising tools to its clients at a 10 per cent premium on basic rates.

The bad news is two-fold. First, behavioural techniques are raising the threshold of acceptable standards, leaving traditional channels such as print and television at a disadvantage and potentially accelerating the migration of advertising spend to digital platforms. Second, behavioural techniques require an array of new systems, staff competencies and training to be effective and credible in the marketplace—for example, technologies to dynamically manage web inventory, systems to provide real-time monitoring and support to advertisers, and an online sales force with a deep understanding of the new medium and its value proposition.

From the advertiser's perspective, the online space is still risky and demands a clear justification: despite lower unit costs, it is necessary to spend heavily to achieve sufficient exposure. In addition, it is still unclear whether and in what ways long-form web advertising is effective at brand marketing, especially compared to a 30-second advertising spot on prime-time television or prominent display advertising in national newspapers. News publishers are still struggling to grapple with the new demands of web advertising.

3.6. Whilst the BBC enjoys considerable digital success, there is no evidence that its web presence significantly harms commercial news publishers in the UK

The final goal of this chapter is to think briefly and dispassionately about the effect of the licence-funded BBC on the long-term commercial prospects of UK news publishing in the digital revolution. Clearly, this is a vast, complex and sensitive topic of debate, built upon many substantial prior contributions—notably, from Ofcom and the BBC Trust. We make no definitive claims, but feel that it is critical to our analysis to at least consider the interface between the BBC and the commercial sector. Our research emphasises the following points.

First, it is essential at the outset to recognise that the BBC is an integral component of the UK media landscape. The BBC regularly produces content of critical acclaim and public value that might otherwise remain dormant in a fully commercial market. The BBC's news services, especially, are pivotal to the achievements of public service broadcasting in the UK, and arguably set a global benchmark of success for other countries.

The strength of audience attachment to the BBC brand is consistently underscored during periods of crisis and heightened public awareness—most recently, for example, during the financial crisis (which has propelled the BBC's business correspondent, Robert Peston, into both the limelight and controversy) and the US elections (which underscored the converged capabilities of the BBC, online and offline).[33] Compared to other media sites, the BBC has fared remarkably well on the web. The BBC has built an impressive web presence on the basis of the licence fee. Significantly, it is the only UK media organization to feature in the UK's top 10 web domains (as we described earlier). Each month, its portfolio of 200 individual websites, anchored around bbc.co.uk, attract 12 million UK users and 33 million foreign users. No other UK media site even comes close to those figures.

Second, it is also essential to articulate the concerns that the BBC's success has triggered in the commercial sector. In particular, the success of bbc.co.uk has led a variety of senior media executives, across the entire spectrum of print and broadcast news publishing, to decry its 'rampant' and 'unstoppable' ambitions at complete market dominance.[34] The basic argument is that bbc.co.uk steals audiences that might otherwise have migrated to UK commercial websites, in turn limiting the growth potential of their advertising revenues.

---

[33] http://www.journalism.co.uk/2/articles/532725.php
[34] Phrases used, respectively, by Carolyn McCall (Chief Executive Officer of the Guardian Media Group) and Sir Paul Dacre (editor of the *Daily Mail*).

The issue is compounded by what is regarded as increasingly 'commercial' behaviour by the BBC—indeed, this was a key conclusion of the Burns Report of 2005.[35] In the quest to 'be the best provider of journalism', as Deputy Director-General Mark Byford put it to us, the BBC 'needs to connect with everyone, across all demographics'. Ironically, criticism of the BBC and the licence fee has fuelled its efforts to engage the audience, particularly amongst the younger generation.

The commercial sector generally views this imperative as deeply anti-competitive: the BBC is using the force of public funds to dominate the entire UK audience, even as it fragments into a multiplicity of digital niches. It was no surprise, therefore, that the 48 per cent budgetary overspend on bbc.co.uk in 2007/8 was seized upon by media executives as evidence that the BBC lacked a sufficient degree of financial accountability and managerial oversight. Although the BBC spends just 3 per cent of its public funding on the web, a budgetary overrun of this magnitude would indeed be problematic in the commercial sector, where publishers are struggling to cover the basic costs of their digital operations.[36] In a recent speech to the Society of Editors, Sir Paul Dacre (Editor of the *Daily Mail*) captured something of the commercial sentiment towards the BBC:

> *Something must be done about my favourite bête noire: the ever growing ubiquity of the BBC. For make no mistake, we are witnessing the seemingly inexorable growth of what is effectively a dominant state-sponsored news service. The corporation has all but seen off ITV's news services, both nationally and locally, has crippled commercial radio, is distorting the free market for internet news-papers and now, with its preposterous proposal for 65 ultra local websites, is going for the jugular of the local newspaper industry. Lines must be drawn in the sand.*[37]

Third, these criticisms rely on opinion rather than evidence-based assertions. The reality is that there is no credible economic evidence to indicate that the success of bbc.co.uk significantly reduces the digital revenues of its commercial rivals.[38] In a detailed review of the BBC's online presence, the Graf Report of 2004 was unable to prove or disprove whether bbc.co.uk had adversely impacted competition by deterring commercial

---

[35] http://www.parliament.the-stationery-office.com/pa/ld200506/ldselect/ldbbc/50/5004.htm

[36] In 2006–7, for example, the BBC allocated just 3% of the licence fee to bbc.co.uk, compared to 70% on television channels and 17% on radio services.

[37] http://www.pressgazette.co.uk/story.asp?storycode=42394

[38] See also http://www.bbc.co.uk/bbctrust/research/economic_impact/trust_conclusions.html

investment in similar services.[39] The official view, espoused by Ofcom, is that the BBC's direction of innovation—for example, the on-demand iPlayer application or high-definition television—is unlikely to have a negative impact on the wider market.

Due to the rapid pace of innovation, however, and the difficulties of predicting consumer behaviour, Ofcom admits that its model of market impact assessment is only partial. It is impossible to know with any certainty exactly how any proposed change in the BBC's service will affect the dynamics of the market. In its recent review of the iPlayer, for example, Ofcom cautioned:

> *Market complexities and the rapid pace of technological change in this market limit the value a consumer survey can add towards assisting with assessing the market impact of iPlayer. The vast majority of the general public struggle with the technology and terminology involved, with some of the iPlayer components being well outside their current range of experiences—and even imagination. This makes it very difficult for them to respond meaningfully to hypothetical questions—such as the effect using the imagined service might have on their consumption patterns.*[40]

Nonetheless, the international evidence suggests that the public value of BBC news is likely to significantly outweigh any negative market impact. Across the world, in markets of all varieties, the commercial news media are struggling to generate revenue from the web, even in countries that lack a public service broadcast equivalent of the BBC (such as the US). It is fallacious, therefore, to suggest that the BBC is a significant factor in the difficulties that commercial publishers are facing in generating revenues from their websites.

Fourth, the public funding of BBC news can also be defended from a civic perspective. Audience research consistently indicates that viewers and listeners value the BBC's news services: and that means that they tend to turn to it rather than foreign-based websites. Indeed, many US citizens also have come to regularly use the BBC and other UK-based websites—such as the *Guardian* and the *Daily Mail*—both of which, at different ends of the left–right spectrum, show the value of a clear editorial line as against the more balanced and neutral aspect of US newspaper sites.

---

[39] http://news.bbc.co.uk/1/hi/entertainment/3866355.stm
[40] http://www.ofcom.org.uk/research/tv/bbcmias/ondemand/bbc_ondemand/bbciplayersurvey/

Without the BBC, citizens (especially from the younger generation) might choose to shun the news entirely, in favour of 'stickier' spaces of sociability and fantasy. As such, it is erroneous to assume that the UK citizen would enjoy a more plural and competitive news media without the presence of the BBC. As Professor Patrick Barwise observed to us:

Any suggestion that reducing or curtailing the BBC's national and international news activities (on- or offline) would, by eliminating or decreasing this crowding out, increase the quality, credibility or value for money of national/international news available to UK citizens would obviously be nonsense.

Fifth, there is, nonetheless, a clear *decoupling* between the BBC's spending capability and the experience of the commercial sector, where diminishing revenues and profits are projected to cause further reductions in spending.[41] In its 2007 review, *New News, Future News*, for example, Ofcom calculated that, with the exception of Channel 5, the direct income generated by national news programming on both ITV and Channel 4 was sufficient to cover only 48 and 70 per cent (respectively) of the direct costs of producing that programming.[42] Hence, the majority of national news output on the terrestrial commercial channels is loss-making. As noted, Sky News is also unprofitable and depends upon a cross-subsidy from BSkyB: our research indicates that Sky's direct news income covers just 30 per cent of its direct cost base. The decoupling effect is also evident in the UK radio market, where the BBC accounts for 55 per cent of listeners.[43] Ofcom estimates that BBC radio is now outspending commercial radio by approximately £135 million.[44]

However, it is also worth noting that the public value delivered by the BBC is also subject to funding constraints, albeit to a lesser extent than in the commercial sector. In 2007, the BBC received £3.4 billion in public funding from the licence fee, in addition to other forms of government support (both of which are under review), as well as commercial revenues from its international arm.[45] The BBC has also had to implement substantial cost savings across its news division, as a result of a lower than anticipated

---

[41] http://www.ft.com/cms/s/0/88359750-b76e-11dd-8e01-0000779fd18c.html

[42] Ofcom, *New News, Future News: The Challenges for Television News after Digital Switchover*, 2007: http://www.ofcom.org.uk/research/tv/reports/newnews/

[43] Ofcom, *The Communications Market*, 2008: http://www.ofcom.org.uk/research/cm/cmr08/

[44] http://www.ofcom.org.uk/research/cm/cmr08/radio/

[45] According to Mark Byford (Deputy Director-General), BBC Global News is currently operating at a loss; in 2007, sales were £39.8 million, compared to costs of £54.6 million. It is forecast to break even in 2010.

rise in the licence fee. That is leading to job cuts in both newsgathering and the newsroom, as well as cuts to the fees awarded to freelance correspondents and producers. As such, there is also an important degree of overlap in the behaviour of the BBC and the commercial sector: both are pursuing more agile, cost-efficient models of gathering, processing and delivering the news.

To be sure, the BBC is using its resource base to maintain and even extend certain aspects of newsgathering. Significantly, the BBC is seeking to implement cost savings of 3–4 per cent per annum in newsgathering, versus 5 per cent in the newsroom. According to Peter Horrocks (Head of the BBC Newsroom), that was a deliberate strategic choice by BBC management 'to prioritise content generation over content processing'. That too is matched by similar behaviour in the commercial sector, where some publishers are funnelling cost savings from the newsroom into expanded coverage. In fact, global media businesses such as News Corporation overshadow the resource capabilities of the BBC. The point, therefore, is that the public funding of the BBC does not automatically grant it creative superiority or immunity from wider cost pressures.

Finally, the development of the BBC's web presence should be shaped in a fashion that not only minimises the risk of any market distortion, but also maximises the potential for collaboration and coexistence between the BBC and the commercial sector. We deal with each of these issues in turn.

The dangers of market distortion are perhaps most vivid in the local and regional market, where the BBC has expressed a strong desire to implement a network of regionally focused, on-demand web video news channels (estimated to cost approximately £68 million over five years). Commercial publishers, especially local newspapers, viewed this as a serious threat at a time when they were anyway under great pressure from loss of advertising and circulation.

In a recent statement to a House of Commons Select Committee for Culture, Media and Sport, both Carolyn McCall (Chief Executive of Guardian Media Group) and Sly Bailey (Chief Executive of Trinity Mirror)— whose companies have large networks of local and regional newspapers— stated the BBC's plans would put regional newspapers under immense strain, resulting in more closures and a virtual BBC monopoly in many markets around the UK. For example, Trinity Mirror has already closed 44 local and regional titles in 2008. In this case, the market impact would appear to significantly outweigh any public value, as McCall emphasised:

Margins in the regional press are being squeezed very hard and the issue for me is significant, not just for me because I'm a publisher but because I think this is a danger to plurality, diversity and democracy.[46]

Recognising this danger, the BBC Trust ruled in late November that the BBC should not pursue its plan to launch a network of ultra-local news websites, and that the allocated £68 million should instead be used to improve existing local and regional news services.[47] An independent analysis by Ofcom similarly suggested that the BBC's proposals would have a 'significant negative impact on commercial providers', potentially reducing their annual revenues by up to 4 per cent.[48]

This was the first time that the application of a Public Value Test by the BBC (which is always informed by a Market Impact Assessment conducted by Ofcom) came out against the expansion of the BBC's service—and reflects both a more careful eye on resources, and a more wary sense that the 'crowding out' argument is gathering traction. The decision represents a significant drawback for the BBC, which has been rapidly expanding its presence on the web. In effect, the decision is a clear statement that the local and regional online market is now off limits to the BBC, potentially creating breathing space for the commercial sector to develop web-based sources of news.

In the long term, quite how the interface between the BBC and the commercial sector will be managed—from a national to a regional and local scale—is still uncertain. For regulators, the challenge is exploring and devising ways to preserve the public value of the BBC whilst also nurturing a diverse and pluralistic commercial sector of news publishing. For example, in its latest Public Service Broadcasting Review, *Preparing for the Digital Future*, Ofcom emphasised that 'no single institution can be equally good at meeting all audience needs—a range of providers offers different kinds of content to meet different audience needs'.[49] Similarly, in a recent interview, Lord Stephen Carter (the UK's first Minister for Communications, Technology and Broadcasting) noted:

---

[46] http://www.guardian.co.uk/media/2008/nov/04/bbc-pressandpublishing
[47] http://www.bbc.co.uk/bbctrust/news/speeches/ml_statement.html
[48] http://www.ofcom.org.uk/media/news/2008/11/nr_20081121
[49] Ofcom, *Second Public Service Broadcasting Review: Preparing for the Digital Future* (2008), p. 36: http://www.ofcom.org.uk/consult/condocs/psb2_phase2/

If it is the case that, in a fully digital world, the market does not find itself able to produce the sort of independent, impartial news that we want—nationally, regionally and locally—that is a critically important area of public policy debate that we need to look at. The specific challenge is finding ways to support impartial news— resourced and capable of providing an alternative voice to the excellent service funded by the BBC.[50]

A likely route towards digital coexistence, favoured by the BBC Trust, is to refocus on the characteristics that make bbc.co.uk distinctive and valuable from a public service dimension. The service licence, for example, lists a series of criteria by which the distinctiveness of bbc.co.uk should be assessed, as defined by the BBC Trust (see Table 3.5).

1. BBC editorial values (accuracy, independence, impartiality, taste and decency)
2. Non-commercial (in some genres, such as children's or news, there is particular value in there being no advertising, no subscriptions)
3. Made in, and for, the UK
4. Clear link to television or radio programme brands
5. Level of creative and editorial ambition (seriousness of intent, breadth or depth of subject matter)
6. Fresh and original approach
7. Uniqueness (no one else provides this content)

Table 3.5. Distinctiveness criteria for assessment of bbc.co.uk

Central to the philosophy of the service licence is the view that the BBC should act as a 'trusted guide'; a 'starting point on the internet, guiding users to the wider web and linking to external websites with high public value'.[51] As noted by Ian Hunter, Managing Editor of BBC Internet: 'we are in a hugely privileged position and should attempt to share out traffic across other publishers'.

In practice, however, the volume of click-through traffic from bbc.co.uk to external sites is believed to be trending downwards, according to the most recent study by the BBC Trust.[52] That is largely due to the ineffectiveness and inaccessibility of links on the existing site. For example, there is still relatively little use of embedded hyperlinks within news stories; unlike sites such as Wikipedia, bbc.co.uk relegates links to the side of the page, making navigation more difficult for readers.

---

[50] http://www.bbc.co.uk/radio4/factual/mediashow/mediashow_20081105.shtml
[51] BBC Trust, 'Service Review of bbc.co.uk' (2008), p. 49:
http://www.bbc.co.uk/bbctrust/framework/bbc_service_licences/bbc_co_uk.html
[52] Ibid., p. 52.

In our view, what this underscores is the need for qualitatively new systems and training that inculcate a more open and collaborative approach to the writing, presentation and cross-referencing of news stories on the web. For the BBC, such an approach will arguably be key to providing public value and meeting its service licence criteria. Such an approach is also vital to the future of commercial news publishers, who are relying on new journalistic skills (oriented around hyperlinking and search engine optimization) to capture web audiences, and to the future of an informed citizenry (as we explain in the conclusion to the report).

4. The sources of news

The commercial pressures facing publishers are enhancing the appeal and practical importance of external suppliers of news and information. As news publishers of all sizes seek to rein in the cost of their newsgathering, both domestically and internationally, the temptation to process rather than generate content becomes more intense. To feed the appetite of 24/7 media platforms, news publishers simply require much more content than they can generate on their own—the exceptions to this trend being the remaining newspapers (often specialist in their content) with global reach, such as the *Financial Times* and *The Economist*, or the BBC, which, by virtue of its resource base and public service mandate, will 'never be a wire service—and will always invest in creating quality content' (Mark Byford, Deputy Director-General, BBC).

For other publishers, though, wire agencies such as Associated Press and Reuters are an increasingly critical element of the digital transition as they provide access to a trusted and geographically extensive newsgathering operation, which is adept at generating text, video and photography. It is hardly a surprise, therefore, that news publishers have oscillated between *wire zero* and *wire plus* in their editorial process. The former essentially regurgitates information from the wires, with little if any additional value being added. The latter supplements the underlying information with a smattering of extra ingredients (ranging from a particular editorial slant, to additional comments and analysis).

Across the industry, cost pressures are increasing the role and appeal of these trusted wholesalers. The wire services have long been a vital source of information and contextual orientation: breaking news—especially internationally—tends to originate from the wires, depending upon the location and availability of correspondents. Through a network of overlapping deals and strategic partnerships, the wires also provide subscribers with access to news at a local and regional scale. Now, however, that relationship is becoming one of greater dependence.

Access to the newsgathering capabilities of the wire agencies does come at a cost. In several interviews, editors expressed concern at the recent inflation of wire subscription fees. The Associated Press, for example, has logically sought to increase subscription charges from newspapers and broadcasters for the digital reuse of its material. It is also planning to enforce a controversial new rate structure, starting in 2009 (a move that recently prompted Tribune, one of the largest US-based newspaper publishers, to cancel its AP subscription).[53]

In a series of lawsuits, AP has also moved to enforce its copyrights across the web, as illustrated by its landmark case against VeriSign's news aggregation service, Moreover.com, in 2007. Information from the wires is likely to become more not less commoditised. Google News, for example, now allows consumers to directly access the wire material that underpins coverage in the mainstream media—a move that has the potential to 'disintermediate' (bypass) publishers, or at least those that add limited value to the underlying body of commoditised information. As such, the relationship between the wires and news publishers is being strengthened but also redefined by the digital revolution.

Importantly, the digital revolution is also cementing new connections between publishers and alternative suppliers of news. It is this issue that forms the focus of the present chapter. In particular, news publishers are increasingly looking for stories, leads and information from two areas: first, the specialist communications experts and public relations agencies that now mediate access to most branches of government, commercial, charitable and scientific activity; and second, the new army of citizen journalists—equipped with an arsenal of camera phones, wireless devices and laptops—which increasingly provides publishers with a shortcut to the front line of breaking stories. We examine each in turn.

[53] http://www.dmwmedia.com/news/2008/10/17/tribune-gives-notice-drop-associated-press-content

4.1. The PR industry now plays a powerful and pivotal role in the gathering, packaging and distribution of news and information

The art of public relations is by no means unique to the present age. The packaging and selective targeting of information to publishers of news can be traced back to the nineteenth century, when the combined forces of mass industrialization, mass rail transit and mass consumption created a newspaper market through which individuals, companies and organizations could, for the first time, communicate with a national audience. In turn, the age of the mass media accelerated the development of a sophisticated public relations industrial complex, which was specifically designed to shape and manage the flow of specialist information into the public sphere.

The digital revolution must be understood against this historical backdrop. Although it has a clear lineage, the PR industry is now assuming a critical and contested role in the gathering and distribution of news—in a broadly defined sense, to include events, processes and initiatives of public interest.

Amidst the churn of the 24/7, multi-channel media environment, communications and public relations skills are of paramount importance— not only to profit-seeking businesses and image-conscious government departments, but also to charities, trade bodies, non-governmental organizations and individuals (activists, celebrities, politicians, etc.) who occupy prominent positions in public life. For organizations and individuals to successfully launch and sustain a message across a range of media platforms, they now need access to a PR machine of some form.

Entering the unpredictable waters of the media without the guidance of a PR specialist is, as one interviewee wryly observed, as ill advised as 'going to court without a lawyer'. But it is not simply about reputation management: from a regulatory standpoint, PR is also pivotal. PR offers clients a structured, professional and trusted approach to communications, thereby ensuring compliance with the various regulations that affect different sectors of economic and social activity.

Demand for PR services has mushroomed: the UK sector as a whole now employs over 30,000 media-facing professionals, generating in excess of £6 billion each year.[54] The sector comprises a diverse array of firms, stretching from boutique consultancies to global PR agencies, who package everything from consumer products to the political rationale of war.[55] In

[54] Quoted by Liz Lewis Jones, Director of the Chartered Institute of Public Relations: http://www.cipr.co.uk. Approximately 1/3 of the 30,000 media-facing professionals are members of CIPR.
[55] See N. Davies, *Flat Earth News* (Random House, 2008), ch. 6.

addition, organizations and government agencies typically employ their own PR staff, in the form of press officers and corporate communications executives. Collectively, these two related worlds—stand-alone PR agencies and internal PR departments—produce a vast amount of information (about products, services, initiatives, policies, etc.) that permeates the news agenda on a daily, even hourly basis.

The PR industry now plays a powerful and arguably pivotal role in the gathering and distribution of news. In many accounts, PR has been framed as an inherently negative force, a cancer that is eating away at the heart of modern journalism. Our view is that it is essential and far more productive to understand the inner workings of PR and how it interconnects with the work of journalists. The dichotomy that we find between journalism and PR in recent books such as Nick Davies's *Flat Earth News*, for example, is excessively bleak and misleading.

The PR industry is remarkably diverse in its activities, agenda and outputs, and has a series of benefits. It is through PR that the activities of charities and non-governmental organizations are disseminated to the public: for example, a significant amount of investigative journalism and undercover reporting—on issues ranging from human rights to environmental change and corporate behaviour—now originates from this parallel universe of activism and campaigning, not from the mainstream media. To be sure, there are serious drawbacks to a PR-led media agenda (see below) but there are also reasons for optimism. We advance a balanced analysis, beginning with the economic efficiencies and social welfare gains associated with PR activity.

First, from a purely economic perspective, the emergence of a specialised market sector, devoted to communications and media relations, provides, on aggregate, a more efficient system for the handling and dissemination of information to consumers.[56] Reflecting developments in other industries, PR can be viewed as a form of efficiency-led *vertical disintegration* in the value chain, whereby internal resources are trimmed in favour of external sourcing.[57] Due to commercial pressures, it is no longer feasible for news publishers to maintain an extensive network of newsgathering. In part, the PR industry is filling a vacuum left by the consolidation and integration of newsrooms. PR streamlines the value chain by collapsing the time,

---

[56] See also P. Curtin, 'Re-evaluating Public Relations Information Subsidies: Market-Driven Journalism and Agenda-Building Theory and Practice', *Journal of Public Relations Research,* 11/1 (1999): 53–90.
[57] A related example would be the vertical disintegration of production in the film industry, where in recent decades the Hollywood studios have shed much of their productive capacity in an effort to re-duce costs and enhance their flexibility. In doing so, the studios have become financiers within a web of independent producers and subcontractors.

distance and cost between newsrooms and events of public interest. In fact, the PR industry is becoming increasingly effective at doing so, as recent data from Metrica reveals. In 2007, for example, PR agencies were able to reach 35 per cent of the UK's adult population on average 11 times each month through media coverage.[58]

Second, from a social welfare perspective, the efficiency and sophistication of the PR sector are being harnessed to package and disseminate a vast array of non-commercial, publicly valuable information across society— for example, through updates about regional and national government initiatives, or via a distillation of the latest scientific data, deriving from academia and corporate labs, into a form that informs civic debate and democratic decision-making. The skills of the PR industry are essential to the translation of key messages to non-specialist audiences. The simple reality is that, in the 24/7, multi-channel media environment, the dissemination of news and information is increasingly shaped and enacted by a more eclectic array of organizations and individuals, which reside outside the orbit of the news media.

As a result, the Fourth Estate as it is traditionally understood is being refigured and opened up to a much wider array of participants, including the PR industry—but crucially, without the conscious recognition by PR that it is now a pivotal part of that structure. Despite its benefits, the rise of the PR industry also raises serious questions about the future of accurate, independent and factual journalism. To cover a story, journalists are increasingly referred to PR gatekeepers, rather than the individuals that have a direct stake in the event or announcement. Gavin MacFadyean, Director of the Centre for Investigative Journalism at City University, fears that, when funnelled through the lens of PR, the news media will simply become 'stenographers of the powerful'. As Professor Robert Picard lamented,

> *There is simply too much dependence on pre-packaged content from PR, and too many quotes from PR spokespeople. That detaches news from its context and filters the event through their lens. News is weaker without the comment of actual figures and decision-makers.*

---

[58] See the report, http://www.metrica.net/MeasurementMatters/post/2008/04/Metrica-Numbers-2007—-PR-benchmark-data-available-now!.aspx

And given the strength of the ties that bind PR experts to their clients or employers, there are reasons to doubt the authenticity and veracity of stories, surveys or announcements that originate from press officers and communications consultants. Crucially, the market-oriented imperatives that guide PR do not always necessarily align with the public interest or an ethos of balanced, objective reporting.[59] The emphasis is always with the needs of the client.

The influence of PR in the area of health reporting is illustrative; for example, big pharmaceutical companies often suppress stories that cast a negative light on their drugs, or organise community events, pseudo-surveys and initiatives that foster the creation of new disorders and new products. As Martin Moore (Director of the Media Standards Trust) described, 'one of the big problems is when the interest of journalists and PR agents coincide but potentially compromise the interests of the public'.

A vivid example of the social impacts of PR-led reporting was the powerful media campaign surrounding the breast cancer drug Herceptin. In this particular case, the confluence of PR consultants, affected patients and uncritical journalists all conspired to change government policy—resulting in the provision of a highly expensive drug on the NHS, and by default, the diversion of funds away from alternative forms of treatment, such as longer term palliative care.[60] Speaking about disease awareness campaigns more generally, Dr Ben Goldacre, a general practitioner and columnist for the *Guardian*, has argued that the growing dependence of journalists on health-related PR is damaging objectivity and contributing to the 'medicalization of society':

> *Disease awareness campaigns ... can be very valuable, but the reality is that [they] are run by pharmaceutical companies generally to sell their own drug. Now sometimes that's a very specific and obvious thing because it's a disease that can only be treated by their drug ... Sometimes it's a disease that was invented by the company—like female sexual dysfunction. The medicalization of society has expanded to everyday life in a way that many people would consider inappropriate like social anxiety disorder or restless leg syndrome or even night eating syndrome. It's simply an opportunity to sell SSRI anti depressant drugs. (Speaking at the Westminster Media Forum, 1 July 2008)*

[59] See J. McManus, 'A Market-Based Model of News Production', *Communication Theory*, 5/4 (1995): 301–38.
[60] http://www.guardian.co.uk/society/2006/aug/23/health.comment

The risk of a serious misalignment between the private interests of PR clients and the public interest of society could be minimised, to some extent, by the presence of regulations and industry-led codes of conduct. In the health sector, for example, the Association of British Pharmaceutical Industries seeks to ensure that public announcements made by member companies are factual and balanced, but in practice tends to lack teeth in some aspects of its enforcement activities.

It is also in the long-term commercial interests of the PR industry to foster best practice. We found that in certain sections of the market, notably at the larger and more reputable PR firms, announcements and studies underwent a rigorous series of checks and quality-control measures before being released into the public domain. In fact, codes of conduct are arguably more clearly defined and observed by PR firms than certain newspapers. For example, the Chartered Institute of Public Relations operates a strict code of conduct—designed to foster ethical and transparent behaviour—that serves to differentiate members from non-members. That code also underpins and reinforces the trust that journalists invest in particular PR firms. Similarly, members of the Public Relations Consultants Association are bound by a professional code of conduct.

A common misconception, therefore, is that the underlying mission of PR is at odds with basic values such as accuracy, honesty and transparency. Like any industry sector, PR is characterised by a spectrum of behavioural tendencies; at one end, there are firms that observe strict codes of conduct; whilst at another end there are firms that consistently engage in morally suspect activities. Equally, news publishers diverge in their approach and overall ethos towards the use of PR material. Martin Moore framed the issue as follows:

> *The long-term challenge is not simply how to make journalism more transparent about its many sources, which necessarily include PR feeds, but also how to convince non-media organizations such as PR firms that they too have a social responsibility to be honest in their reporting of the world.*

4.2. The mutual exchange of information between journalists and PR is dependent on relationships of trust and credibility

In practice, the interface between journalists and PR is more symbiotic than other commentators have hitherto suggested. It is not a simple case of PR material flowing unchecked into the willing hands of time-starved journalists, although that does increasingly occur. Rather, the process is best viewed as one of reciprocal engagement and mutual exchange, which is refracted by the personal relationships that connect individuals in the two spheres of activity.

On the one hand, there is evidence of PR professionals pushing material into the hands of journalists; notably, by targeting announcements and press releases to specific individuals, media channels and audiences. We found that PR firms and in-house PR departments alike have sought to become more efficient and targeted in their communications with journalists. Today, that process relies heavily upon the internet: news wires, email lists, really simple syndication feeds (RSS) and social networking groups ensure that journalists are bombarded with a digital tsunami of information every day.

In some quarters, notably the regional press, the adoption of PR material has been faster and more flagrant: Nick Davies's evidence for this seems well grounded. However, his portrait of an industry whose products flow seamlessly into the news chain is exaggerated: inserting PR information into the media agenda is still fraught with difficulty and is certainly not as straightforward as he implies. PR messages compete for exposure, which accentuates the importance of personal relationships of trust (see below), as well as internal checks and quality controls—a point made by a senior PR executive:

> *We now quality-test, pre-digest and stress-test material before we try it on the media ... Even with time pressures, and being behind desks, news organisations are hardened places, and they need to keep up the ratings ... So we still have to work hard to get our stories out there.*

Yet the difficulties of achieving media exposure mean that PR material is frequently hyped or worse, manipulated, to whet the appetites of journalists and editors. PR will also spin a story to attract the attention of consumers. In one vivid example, described to us anonymously, a PR firm was hired by a US client to help it sell surplus stock of plastic storage boxes; the PR team then created a news story linked to the prevailing fears of radiation and dirty bombs, stating that such boxes were a way of protecting belongings. The client had sold the surplus stock by the next day.

In the course of our research, we have spoken with a broad spectrum of individuals and organizations which rely upon PR expertise to manage their communication needs. The consensus view is that the interface between PR and the media is a fertile breeding ground for sensationalism (see also Chapter 7). PR professionals have the skills to package their content, whilst newsrooms are looking for content that can boost ratings, audiences and ultimately, advertising revenues.

We found that charities and NGOs, in particular, are under growing pressure to sensationalise their message—namely, through shocking revelations and/or celebrity endorsements. The danger of this trend is that the media agenda is shaped and populated by those with the requisite PR skills. The following comments were made by policy and news chiefs from leading UK charities:

> *The Daily Mail actually said to us, 'You are not saying anything shocking enough. You are not saying what the government is doing wrong'. They want blame. Those stories always get picked up.*

> *The celebrity culture has really put pressure on charities to go down that route. If we don't have a celebrity figure that will go out there for us, we just aren't going to get our message across.*

> *It is not about the 'worthiness' of a story; it is simply about what sells … Celebrities are important to raise our profile … [They are] highly significant, and give you access to the mass market.*

On the other hand, there is also evidence of journalists pulling material from PR professionals for specific areas of coverage. For reasons we will discuss later, journalists are under growing pressure to produce more content, for a wider range of platforms. By default, that means that journalists have less time to conduct original research or explore issues in significant depth. It is no surprise, therefore, that journalists increasingly turn to PR for comment, expert analysis and research.

The appeal of PR is magnified, to varying degrees, by their proven skills in packaging, targeting and tracking content. This is especially evident in the area of broadcast video, where clips produced by PR firms now regularly penetrate the news agenda. The UK Home Office, for example, regularly commissions television producers from ITN and Sky to create documentaries related to issues such as policing and immigration. A leading example of this trend is the PR agency Media Link, which produces video news releases (VNRs) for clients and then seeds that content into broadcast newsrooms across the UK (including the BBC and all other major publishers). Because of embedded Teletrax watermarking technology, deployed in partnership with Philips, we know that in 2007 Media Link VNRs achieved over 60 hours of television exposure across Europe.

Media Link is able to seed its VNRs on the basis of high production qualities and close relationships with editors and executives at news publishers. With an established track record in targeting, measuring and assessing the impact of their messages amongst specific demographic groups, PR firms such as Media Link are not only crucial to individuals and organizations seeking favourable media coverage; they are also a valuable resource to audience-hungry news publishers. In addition, news feeds from PR are appealing to news publishers because they are free, and can generally be relied upon to generate content on otherwise slow days. PR chiefs confirmed to us that television newsrooms frequently call to source softer, more celebrity-oriented stories (particularly to fill space on the latest news websites).

The symbiosis between journalists and PR professionals also rests upon individual relationships of trust and credibility. The tyranny of computer-based working—which increasingly ties journalists to their desks, and exposes them to a constant stream of impersonal press releases—enhances the value and impact of personal recommendations and contacts. 'Reputation is vital', notes Liz Lewis-Jones (Director of CIPR), not least because of the volume of PR messages that now bombard time-pressured journalists every day.

PR professionals work to cultivate relationships with the journalists and editors that will not only guarantee exposure but will also imbue a layer of legitimacy upon the story. Their measurement of success is still largely rooted in the scarcity of broadcast and print, as opposed to the abundance of the web. The media agenda is still driven by prominent shows, anchored by star personalities such as John Humphrys, Andrew Marr or Jeremy Paxman, or by influential columns, penned by the likes of Martin Wolf at the *FT* or Simon Jenkins at the *Guardian* and *The Times*. Exposure within these channels continues to command far more respect than pure online news coverage.

The relationships that underpin the interface between journalism and PR are deepening and diversifying due to an ongoing flow of talent from the former to the latter. Notably, we have found evidence of a *brain drain* effect, brought about by the migration of successful editors, journalists and other commentators from newsrooms into PR agencies and corporate communications roles.[61] The recent appointment of Peter Barron, former editor of BBC *Newsnight*, as head of communications and public affairs at Google UK is certainly emblematic of this shift.[62] Journalists are valuable to PR precisely because of their newsroom experience; their knowledge of how to position a story, who to call to get exposure, how to bargain with other 'hacks' and so on.

Quantifying the speed or extent of the brain drain is difficult, but the economic rationale is certainly clear. In the view of Simon Walker, a PR veteran, the lure of generous salaries and other perquisites mean that journalism is increasingly viewed as a temporary 'stepping stone' to a more lucrative career in a communications-oriented sector.[63] According to recent data from the National Union of Journalists, for example, nearly 50 per cent of all journalists earn less than the average wage in the UK. In 2005, the average salary of a junior reporter and editor was £20,780 and £39,800 respectively. By comparison, *PR Week* estimates that average entry-level salaries in the PR sector are now over £29,000, whilst average salaries at CEO and board director level are approaching £70,000.[64] The long-term challenge for news publishers, therefore, is how best to retain talent and preserve the dynamism of the newsroom.

As we discuss later, investing in star journalists and celebrity commentators is a potential response, not least to retain influence over the wider media agenda and also to differentiate the news brand on digital platforms. For Jim Doherty, President of the NUJ, however, the flow of talent from journalism into PR is set to continue for the foreseeable future:

---

[61] The brain drain also operates at an earlier phase in the career path of journalists; through the diversion of graduates from journalism courses to PR-related courses at college and university. There has been significant growth in the latter courses in recent years.

[62] http://www.pressgazette.co.uk/story.asp?sectioncode=1&storycode=41796&c=1

[63] In practice, there may be a series of stepping stones; for example, we have found evidence that specialist correspondents are moving into trade publications, where they have the time and resources to focus on particular kinds of coverage (e.g. science, business). Even there, however, the financial lure of PR remains strong.

[64] http://www.prweek.com/uk/reports/surveys

Over the last few years, the older, experienced journalists, who perhaps cost a little bit too much money, have [increasingly] been made redundant and perhaps then moved into PR where they have the time and the expertise to shape the policies and promote them ... We are essentially left with a young and underpaid collection of journalists ... Therefore the tipping point will continue to go in favour of more media relations and more PR. (Speaking at the Westminster Media Forum, 1 July 2008)

Overall, we view the PR industry as an integral component of the media landscape, and as a pivotal agent in the gathering, packaging and dissemination of news to consumers. The symbiosis between journalism and PR can be argued to deliver economic efficiencies and social welfare gains; but it also underscores the need for more transparency among journalists in the sourcing of news, not least to identify areas of coverage where the private interests of PR may collide with the public interest of objective reporting. Martin Moore of the Media Standards Trust emphasised to us that it is now time 'to critically engage with that reality—the nexus of PR and journalism—rather than attack it outright and hark back to a mythical era of independence'. We support that view and later in the report outline potential initiatives that might enable a greater degree of transparency in the sourcing and processing of news, particularly from the PR sector. The open source tags, pioneered by the MST, are a powerful example of the flexible self-description that the internet can bring to journalism (see Chapter 8).

4.3. The digital revolution is transforming the audience into co-producers and co-distributors of news and other information

At the heart of the digital revolution is a confluence of hardware and software technologies, which are collectively making it easier and cheaper for individuals—professionals as well as amateurs—to record, store and distribute content of all kinds. A plethora of new digital technologies— digital cameras, smart phones, cheaper computers, broadband connections, wi-fi connections, blogs, social media websites, search engines—are enabling audiences to take a more active role in the gathering, analysis and coverage of news events. Blogging software, especially, has dramatically simplified the publication of content via the web; and is analogous to the transformative impact of print media in the fifteenth century, which unshackled the written word from the time and cost of manual inscription.

Today, however, the rise of citizen journalism is being driven not only by technological possibility, but also by an array of other incentives; for example, the prospect of monetary rewards, the pursuit of self-expression, engagement with like-minded individuals, or the simple satisfaction of filling gaps in the news agenda.

The resulting torrent of 'user-generated content' (UGC) poses distinct challenges for news publishers, which have traditionally been organised on a linear basis as purveyors of packaged news, which was sent to a relatively passive audience, via broadcast or print. That mass-media model is now giving way to a more interactive and more democratised model, which instead rests upon an ongoing and expansive conversation with the online audience. As Iain Martin (Associate Editor of Comment at the *Daily Telegraph*) noted: 'The old idea of newspapers handing down tablets of stone to a grateful public is giving way to a more democratised model of production.'

News coverage of recent disasters revealed the new importance of the citizen journalist. Writing on his blog about the impact of the tsunami on Sri Lanka in December 2004, Tom Glocer (Chief Executive Officer, Thomson Reuters) noted:

> *For the first 24 hours the best and the only photos and video came from tourists armed with telephones, digital cameras and camcorders. And if you didn't have those pictures, you weren't on the story.*[65]

Having the capability to harness the insights and experience of the audience is increasingly vital to news publishers. It not only provides a short cut to the front line of unfolding events—which reporters may otherwise be unable to reach in time—it also helps to build a community around a brand and thereby improve the *social stickiness* of the website. As the success of the *Guardian*'s 'Comment is Free' attests, news publishers can quickly and cheaply populate their websites with colourful, wide-ranging views from the audience. Technology writer Nicholas Carr views the recent embrace of UGC as 'sharecropping in disguise': a way for companies to profit from the rise of digital volunteerism on the web.[66]

[65] http://tomglocer.com/blogs/sample_weblog/archive/2006/10/11/98.aspx
[66] http://www.roughtype.com/archives/2006/12/sharecropping_t.php

In a recent study of citizen journalism, John Kelly (a reporter from the *Washington Post*, and visiting fellow of Oxford's Reuters Institute) examined the generic interactive features that UK news publishers are now adopting to expand their pool of user-generated content.[67] Notable examples include polls (eliciting answers to topical questions), comments and message boards (allowing users to leave remarks next to a story or specified topic) and galleries of user-generated content (with photos, video and other media).

Achieving these kinds of interactivity, however, is actually a complex and, crucially, a resource-intensive process for news publishers. To effectively manage the relationship with the audience, news publishers require specialist teams that have the time, expertise and systems to monitor, moderate and edit contributions, especially for discussions around more controversial topics. In fact, it may be cheaper and more efficient for news publishers to outsource that work to external partners, in a similar fashion to the efficiency-led vertical disintegration that has increased the appeal of PR news feeds. Reflecting this approach, *The Times* has decided to outsource its web monitoring to a specialist firm, e-Moderation. A possible danger in outsourcing moderation is that it distances the newsroom from the subtleties of the online conversation. Whether internal or external, however, moderation is vital because it enables news publishers to identify and ban abusive or defamatory contributors, or ensure the accuracy and veracity of a particular account.

The screening of user-generated content is essential if it is to be used alongside professional coverage; notably, in the form of eyewitness photos or videos, or the addition of unusual, off-beat stories to the news agenda (e.g. the 'Your News' slot on Channel 5, 'Oddly Enough' at Thomson Reuters). However, searching for the diamonds in the rough of web comments can ultimately add value to the news product:

> *We have to polish UGC to some extent. Some of the message boards—e.g. Have your Say—are unmoderated. Most of the controversial ones are moderated; and that's what takes up the greatest effort. We also extract the best bits of information from UGC, adding quotes to the news stories—where there are germane contributions from the audience, becoming part of the story itself. (Peter Horrocks, Head of BBC Newsroom)*

[67] J. Kelly, *Red Kayaks and Hidden Gold: The Rise, Challenges and Value of Citizen Journalism* (Reuters Institute for the Study of Journalism, Oxford University, forthcoming, 2009). Adapted from A. Hermida and N. Thurman, 'A Clash of Cultures: The Integration of User-Generated Content within a Professional Journalistic Framework at British Newspaper Websites', paper presented to the Future of Newspapers Conference, Cardiff University, Wales, 12–13 Sept. 2007.

At present, news publishers are still grappling with the longer term implications of citizen journalism, and how best to manage the online conversation. It is still unclear, for example, whether the inclusion of citizen journalism features adds any significant value to the brand or to the advertising value of the website—making decisions about ongoing resource allocation especially difficult. Deciding how far to invest in the medium, and what role to give the audience in the publishing process, are thorny issues that confront all news publishers, as Horrocks described:

> *Everything is technically possible online, but the key question is to what extent we can allocate resources to meet all those demands. The BBC has a remit to be universal, so we have to carefully distinguish between what we can do and what we should do.*

There is an underlying fear throughout the UK's media group boardrooms and newsrooms that, by opening up the publishing process to the digital audience too far or too soon, news brands may be in danger of diluting existing editorial values, or tarnishing the product with a cacophony of confusing voices. Participation in citizen journalism is still highly asymmetric, with the result that interactive features may be distorted or hijacked by a vocal minority of digitally literate users. It is estimated that only 1 per cent of website visitors actually interact with a news website; for example, by uploading content or leaving a comment. There is a frequent disparity, moreover, between the 'most read' stories and stories that attract the 'most comments'.

The emergence of citizen journalism therefore raises serious questions about the plurality and impartiality of interactive news websites and the broader news agenda. It also raises a series of ethical questions, relating to media regulations about accuracy, privacy and libel, which are likely to surface as news publishers navigate the new terrain of user-generated content.

In the course of our research, we discovered a keen awareness of these issues among editors and journalists. However, we also found that editorial rhetoric increasingly diverges from the pressures and practicalities of the digital revolution. The ascendance of the audience in general, and the clickstream in particular, is increasingly palpable across newsrooms. The tastes of the audience, and the views of citizen journalists, are slowly but surely beginning to reshape the thinking behind news publishing. That is hardly surprising, as the distributed, hyperlinked structure of the web fuels new forms of collective, user-led behaviour and decision-making. From one perspective, the web unleashes the wisdom of crowds; whilst from another, it portends a descent into the mentality of the mob (a distinction we address in Chapter 8).

Evidence of this shift can be glimpsed across the internet—not just in news publishers, but in search engines, aggregators and other branches of the user-oriented 'web 2.0 movement'. The classification and display of stories on Google News, for example, is shaped to a significant extent by the clickstream of consumption. Folksonomies such as Digg or Reddit enable users to vote for stories, creating an online news agenda that is distinctly skewed in its selection. The latest websites such as NewsCred take citizen journalism a step further, by enabling users to vote on the quality and credibility of a story. Concerned by this development, the BBC's Rory Cellan-Jones wrote:

> When I started in this trade a quarter of a century ago, seasoned journalists were confident about two things. They knew which stories were important, and they had strong opinions about which news sources were credible … But in the internet age, a lot of that confidence is seeping away. Editors are increasingly casting a glance at the 'most-read' lists on their own and other websites to work out which stories matter to readers and viewers. And now the audience—which used to know its place—is being asked to act as a kind of journalistic ombudsman, ruling on our credibility.[68]

Plotting the future of citizen journalism—and how it relates to professional journalism—is inherently difficult because of constant changes in its social and technological morphology. In particular, digital technologies have a habit of spawning new and entirely unexpected forms of consumer behaviour. A decade ago, for example, few would have predicted the mass popularity of now-established consumer practices, such as SMS text messaging or peer-to-peer file sharing. Despite this haze of uncertainty, two things are clear: the first is that citizen journalists are playing an increasingly vital role in the new breed of digitally integrated newsrooms; the second, as a corollary, is that the professional journalist is increasingly required to navigate, filter and polish so-called user-generated content, in addition to myriad other information feeds and story leads (e.g. from PR).

We view the rise of citizen journalism as a positive source of change, which has the potential to supplement—not supplant—the professional gathering and coverage of news. In particular, the fusion of user-friendly

---

[68] http://www.bbc.co.uk/blogs/technology/2008/08/credible_news_who_decides.html

web technology with the legal force of Freedom of Information requests has the capacity to reshape the availability of public data, enabling more distributed modes of monitoring and reporting by citizens and other stakeholders, as the varied initiatives of MySociety.org illustrate. The collective power of the web means that complex topics, problems and stories can be assembled, extended and critically evaluated by a distributed workforce of professional and amateurs alike. An especially vivid case study, though from a US context, relates to actions taken by the editor of the Fort Myers News-Press after Hurricane Katrina. After securing local data about relief payments from the Federal Emergency Management Agency, the editor released the entire database online and asked readers to search for possible leads. As Charlie Beckett describes in his recent book, *Super Media*:

> *Within twenty-four hours, 60,000 searches were made throwing up all kinds of leads for the journalists to follow up and publish. Neither journalists nor public could have done this on their own. The combination of skills and resources opened up a story in a way that allowed both to challenge the authorities.*[69]

The implication is that in a more networked and transparent form, which harnesses the knowledge and experience of a varied base of stakeholders, journalism might be able to craft more accurate, meaningful and powerful stories about the world. In that form, news publishers might be able to forge new connections with their audiences; and citizens may be able to make more informed decisions about their life and how best to participate in democratic society.

---

[69] C. Beckett, *Super Media: Saving Journalism So it Can Save the World* (Blackwell, 2008), 54.

5. The digital vision

The digital revolution is forcing news publishers to completely rethink their strategic goals and operational structures. With few exceptions, news publishers are now committed to pursuing a digital vision that is premised upon the logic of integration. At the heart of this strategic and operational transformation is the multimedia newsroom: a state-of-the-art digital hub that is equipped to streamline, process and distribute news stories to audiences through a range of media channels. As a consequence, news publishers are converging upon a central playing field where competition is likely to be intense. Newspapers are diversifying into video and audio, whilst broadcasters are diversifying into the provision of text-based coverage.

In this long-term vision, digital media such as broadband, mobile and even virtual worlds will supplement print and broadcast as sources of news. The underlying goal is to attract a critical mass of audiences (and advertising inventory) around the news and the brand in as many different channels as possible. The rationale for integration is clear: in theory, by funnelling the news through a multimedia hub, news publishers can reduce costs, utilise their content more efficiently in a range of formats and so generate the revenues needed to sustain journalism in the digital revolution. In our view, however, the industry-wide shift towards integration is also imbued with a remarkable degree of myopia and what can be best described as a siege mentality.

We argue in this chapter that news publishers are taking refuge in digital fortresses, but without any systematic quantification of the value of digital audiences or how to achieve meaningful differentiation vis-à-vis their competitors. There is a danger, moreover, that the multimedia newsroom will act as a Trojan horse for new forms of audience-led publishing. As real-time data about the clickstream of digital consumption becomes more visible, we suggest that journalists and publishers alike will be under greater pressure to justify the value and relevance of news stories to the brand and the bottom line. That pressure is likely to be accentuated by the challenge and urgency of securing advertising revenues in the digital media environment.

The clickstream will be especially transformative—perhaps dangerously so—within publishers lacking the shelter of cross-subsidy. In our view, these publishers are in danger of being reduced to the digital equivalent of a *windsock*, shaped by the short-term whims of the news consumer (in an effort to boost hits and advertising) rather than a core of long-term editorial values. In contrast, publishers with the luxury of diversified revenue streams are more likely to consciously navigate the trails of the clickstream by following *editorial isolines*—points of consistent editorial judgement— and hence, invest in the specific content that supports their brand and editorial voice. Over time, we anticipate a growing polarization of the market between these extremes: digital windsocks versus digital anchors.[70]

5.1. The response of publishers is fuelled by a siege mentality, rather than a clear projection and valuation of the digital market

To prepare for the digital revolution, news publishers are increasingly adopting a fully integrated model of production. Typically, that model revolves around a digital hub of some kind: a multimedia news factory designed to be staffed by multi-skilled journalists, and tooled with the latest hardware and software. As one senior media executive observed, there is an almost 'messianic belief—a one way bet—that integration will be the saviour of journalism in the digital revolution'. The model varies significantly between publishers but several core design principles tend to remain constant.

The first is a radial pattern of working in the newsroom, which is typically characterised by a 'hub' (a central editorial desk) and a series of interconnected subject-specific 'spokes' or 'pods'. This design fosters the clustering of expertise around particular subject areas (e.g. business, entertainment, politics, travel) and enables the flow of related content to a range of media platforms. It therefore requires journalists to master different styles of writing (e.g. for the web) and presentation (e.g. for

---

[70] We coined these terms to capture the distinctive characteristics of audience-led versus editorially focused news publishers in the digital revolution.

podcasts or video). In the view of editors, the proximity of teams in the new radial design will facilitate the cross-pollination of ideas between journalists and teams.

The second design principle is the installation of a digital asset management (DAM) platform, such as Avid or Quantel. This is vital to the operation of the multimedia newsroom as it simplifies the gathering, editing and processing of news feeds from different sources. DAM also facilitates the archiving of content and simplifies access to historical data by employees within the organization and by other production partners. Crucially, DAM platforms have enabled news publishers to remove redundant layers of staff from the newsroom—for example, by enabling some journalists to undertake work previously completed by specialists in the newsroom:

> *Investing in technology is a key element for us... Because what it enables us to do is to take out a layer of staff, which is basically craft and production editors, graph editors, etc. It's a new system that enables much more desktop editing by journalists ... Previously, what the journalists would do is come back with their footage, notes and script and go into the editing suite, where it would be put together for them. Now the journalist can do the entire process. (Mark Wood, CEO of ITN)*

A third design principle is web-centricity. Due to the rapid growth of the internet, news publishers are anxious to bring the web into the heart of their operation. Developing a web-centric operation is seen as vital to the future of news brands because of the fragmentation of audiences and the migration of advertising spend. As a result, the latest newsrooms are now equipped to feed the website with content throughout the day and night. In turn, that accentuates the importance of interactivity: newsrooms are also being tooled to process user-generated content and monitor the click-stream of digital consumption. That represents a major paradigm shift for news publishers, who are now struggling to 'think about viewers individually and how best to develop more personalised offerings' (Professor Robert Picard).

The adoption of an integrated newsroom design is a logical response to the challenges of the digital revolution. It is more efficient to process news within a centralised hub, as opposed to a series of individual silos suited to specific channels. That can also yield benefits for the identity and cohesion of the brand; a centralised hub can unify the 'voice' of the brand across different media channels, and indeed across different markets worldwide. Quite where the integrated model will lead news publishers is still unclear: as Alan Rusbridger has observed, a 'journey of exploration is about to begin'. For the National Union of Journalists, that philosophy is concerning: ill-conceived plans are having a clear effect on the working lives of journalists, their health and safety, and on the quality of the work they produce (see next chapter).[71]

What is most surprising, however, is the opacity of the market analysis and decision-making that underpin the redesign and technological upgrade of newsrooms. To be sure, news publishers have spent considerable time and energy studying the best design for their needs and how integration will impact their operation. ITN, for example, produced a series of 'ghost programmes' for six months before finally switching to the new Avid system. Similarly, the *Daily Telegraph* trained its entire editorial staff in a prototype of its flagship newsroom before launching.

But what appears to be missing in the process of integration is a clear sense of how much the digital audience is worth, or indeed how that audience can be monetised in the long term. There is a remarkable lack of clarity in the projection and quantification of the digital market, especially when compared to the metrics that feed into strategic planning and business development in other consumer-facing sectors. The process of integration is premised upon what one interviewee termed 'a siege mentality'; a belief that a well-armed multimedia newsroom will somehow, at some point, generate the audiences and advertising necessary to 'weather the gathering storm'. That view was echoed by another senior media executive:

> There is a general lack of long-term decision-making in strategy; it's about following the pack instead. There is no clear articulation of long-term objective functions; everyone is chasing the ABC demographic quite blindly. This herd mentality creates a dynamic of imitation; whereby everyone follows a first mover; e.g. everyone believes the investment in multimedia newsrooms is the only way to capture audiences online. ... It's a rush into the unknown, rather than a careful, measured response.

Our interviews overwhelmingly support this view. News publishers are committing significant investments to technological upgrades and

---

[71] NUJ *Commission on Multimedia Working* (Dec. 2007), 5:
http://www.nuj.org.uk/innerPagenuj.html?docid=605

sweeping operational changes—without any guarantee of a return or a fully conceptualised sense of direction. Indeed, the character and scale of digital news consumption (as outlined in Chapters 2 and 3) do not appear to offer publishers a strong economic footing. The lure of integration has a series of unintended consequences—namely, the creation of an expensive, complex multimedia hub, which demands skills and resources that are beyond the reach of most news publishers.

5.2. The integration of newsrooms is creating added complexity and is taking publishers beyond their core competencies

The integration of newsrooms will actually create 'complexity rather than simplicity', according to Tim Brooks, Managing Director of Guardian News & Media Group, and will therefore require extra investment in managerial oversight, as well as the training and retraining of staff, as the capabilities of technology evolve. However, it is unlikely that news publishers will have the resources necessary to address this added complexity, or support the ongoing renewal of their technology and skill base. For example, the training budgets of news publishers are generally static or in decline; and typically account for no more than 1–3 per cent of the overall news production budget.

By placing a 'one-way' bet on an integrated future, news publishers face a potentially vicious cycle of resource scarcity and technological obsolescence. In other words, news publishers may find themselves locked into expensive digital fortresses that they cannot afford to fully utilise or maintain.

As we discuss in Chapter 6, there is already clear evidence that publishers are stretching their news budgets—in some cases too far—to meet the increasingly 24/7 demands of multiple media channels. According to one news chief: 'everyone is stretching their resources further frankly: the key debate is how far do you stretch before you fail to fulfil your basic objectives in news provision?' In the course of our research, we found ample evidence that news publishers were struggling to harness the capabilities of their newly integrated operations. At ITN, for example, the staff were only trained to use the essential aspects of the new Avid system during the intensive six-month preparation. In light of the growing pressure on training budgets, it is uncertain when or indeed whether the staff will be trained in the full capabilities of the system. Compounding the situation is the ongoing evolution of the web and related digital technologies. Whilst future generations of journalists are likely to be more comfortable and conversant with the possibilities of the digital era, there is an inevitable time lag between the adoption of technologies by consumers and the systematic incorporation of such technologies into the process of news publishing.

Facing an uncertain future, news publishers cannot afford to regularly train or equip their staff with the tools of the digital revolution. The *Daily Telegraph*, for example, has made a strategic withdrawal from certain digital activities, such as podcasting or *Telegraph PM* (an electronic PDF paper), in order to focus scarce resources around its new web video channel. The web accentuates the problem of resource allocation because it enables news publishers to engage with their audience in a far more dynamic and individualised fashion. Thus, publishers need to balance what is technically possible and what is actually likely to deliver real value. As one newspaper executive observed:

> *We needed to focus and prioritise. It's impossible to achieve every-thing we envisioned online. Like others, we've had to streamline and remain lean due to commercial pressures. It was a strategic decision to focus on video.*

As these examples illustrate, news publishers are migrating far beyond their core competencies in the search for digital success, in turn requiring journalists to cultivate a wide range of new media skills (see also Chapter 6). For newspapers, the transition is especially challenging as they lack the legacy of expertise in audio-visual production that broadcasters enjoy. There is also a critical difference in the production cultures of print versus broadcast newsrooms. The former tend to be characterised by a relatively greater degree of exclusivity and competition than the latter:

> *Online work needs to be more open—to peer review and collabo-ration—than traditional journalism. A certain degree of exclusivity prevails in the print world; for example, keeping big scoops among a small clique. The web demands a more collaborative approach, which can draw on the skills, resources and existing coverage available to the brand. This is analogous to the production model of broadcast, which is oriented around large-scale teams working around a key objective. In my view, this is partly why newspapers have struggled to reposition themselves for the web. (Emily Bell, Director of Digital Content, Guardian)*

In both broadcast and print, however, news publishers believe that they can differentiate themselves through technology. Writing on his popular blog, Buzz Machine, the news media commentator Jeff Jarvis argues that this is a highly irrational move; a rational industry would instead distribute journalists and share digital platforms.[72] For Jarvis, the latest flagship newsrooms are little more than vanity projects—an extension of the industry's well-established 'institutional ego'. In effect, the UK news media is funnelling precious resources into the duplication of systems and digital expertise that others could provide more efficiently:

> *Newspapers should … stop trying to differentiate themselves with technology. Part of the problem is institutional ego. When publishing systems arrived in the 1970s, papers wasted millions of dollars each specing and sometimes building their own customised systems, refusing to admit that what they did—typing, hooking graphs, fitting heads—was no different from any other paper … So take the advice, papers: Get out of the manufacturing and distribution and technology businesses as soon as possible. Turn off the press. Outsource the computers. Outsource the copy-editing to India or to the readers. Collaborate with the reporting public. And then ask what you really are. The answer matters dearly. (July 2008)[73]*

As Jarvis observes, an alternative and arguably more cost-efficient approach would be for news publishers to outsource some of the activities of the multimedia newsroom. That might be to an external technology provider or some variant of a cross-industry initiative, perhaps set up by the BBC or a wire agency such as Associated Press or Thomson Reuters.[74] The underlying goal would be to create a shared technology platform, equipped to provide critical web functions such as search, metadata analysis, video delivery, advertising sales or database services. In fact, there is already tentative evidence of such an approach.

---

[72] The recent cost-cutting measures taken by Independent News and Media (UK) are a step in this direction. From Jan. 2009, INM titles will move from their own premises in London's Docklands to the HQ of Associated Newspapers in Kensington, where they will have dedicated office space and share functions such as information technology, personnel and back office support. The move is expected to deliver savings of £2m–£3m per year for INM. See http://www.independent.co.uk/news/media/press/independent-to-share-with-daily-mail-1039511.html

[73] http://www.buzzmachine.com/tag/journalism/

[74] See a related discussion by Jeff Jarvis at http://www.guardian.co.uk/media/2008/dec/15/digitalmedia-pressandpublishing

In the US, for example, Google has extended its Ad Words auction platform to the print and broadcast sectors, enabling advertisers to buy adverts in selected newspapers, television channels and radio stations. More recently, Google has begun to digitise the archives of over 100 newspaper groups (including the *New York Times* and the *Washington Post*) so that they can be searched via Google News and, eventually, via the websites of the respective news publishers. Under the agreement, Google will place advertising around the archived content and split the revenues with publishers. Positioning itself as the gatekeeper to information of all varieties, Google has constructed an auction platform that can be used to efficiently pair directed search queries with relevant information (news and other content) in real-time.

These developments are significant because they underscore the potential value of strategic collaboration in the digital revolution, not just between publishers and search engines but also across the publishing community. For many news publishers, supplementing their existing web offering with historical content would be a logical next step. Commemorative front pages, or historical summaries (drawing on a range of content), might serve to differentiate the news brand or cement its appeal in particular demographics. Archives could also form part of a premium subscription package, a form of 'walled garden' model that is already used by the *Financial Times*, *The Economist*, and soon, *The Times* under James Murdoch's direction. However, many news publishers are unable to finance the conversion of their archives into searchable databases. For example, ITN faces crippling costs in its development of ITN Source, one of the world's largest commercial video archives:

> For us, ITN Source is about going beyond news to transform ITN into a content company. We have nearly 800,000 hours of footage in the archive; 20,000 hours of which has been digitised. We are currently digitising around 20 hours per day, at a cost of £60 per hour of footage … So it would cost us close to £48 million to convert the entire archive. Right now that sum is too expensive. We have to be very selective about what will add real value to the new media business. (Mark Wood, CEO, ITN)

In theory, our interviewees suggested that the strategic interests of news publishers and Google are in relative alignment. The former are seeking to aggregate audiences and advertising around their content for as long as possible; whilst the latter has immense resources at its disposal to subsidise platforms that will expand the scope of internet use and the size of its advertising network. As technology writer Nicholas Carr notes, 'Google wants information to be free because as the cost of information falls it makes more money'.[75]

Partnering with Google is arguably essential, given its dominance of search and the growing role of search in the navigation of news. It is worth noting, however, that Google effectively depends upon the news publishers and wire agencies for the content that powers its search engine and news aggregator. It is not in Google's long-term interest to erode the economics that sustain the gathering and processing of that content. It is for that reason that Google has simultaneously excluded adverts from its news website and begun to implement revenue-sharing agreements with publishers as it develops advertising-supported news archives.

In practice, however, the relationship between news publishers and Google continues to be fraught with difficulty. Google is ultimately aiming for a sizeable share of the advertising pool around news. Across the media and entertainment industries, Google has struggled to shake its image as a free-rider which continues to profit handsomely from the indexing and navigation of third-party content. In several interviews, Google was portrayed as a *frenemy*—a nimble player that has the capacity to limit as well as enhance the connection between publishers and the audience. Publishers continue to diverge in their strategic appraisal of Google; some have willingly opened their walled gardens to Google's indexing 'bots' (web robots), whilst others have continued to restrict access—notably, by adopting the model of 'first click free'.[76]

5.3. News publishers are in danger of morphing into 'digital windsocks', shaped by the direction of the prevailing clickstream

The opacity of long-term strategic planning arguably enhances the short-term value of the clickstream, both in editorial decision-making and broader strategic discussions. Lacking a clear roadmap, news publishers are more likely to follow the trails of the clickstream in the pursuit of digital success.

That is a logical response to what is still an uncertain and nascent marketplace; but it is also a dangerous path to tread, as many editors and executives admitted to us. The granularity of the clickstream means that

[75] http://www.strategy-business.com/press/article/07404?gko=a2bce-1876-26510326
[76] http://googlewebmastercentral.blogspot.com/2008/10/first-click-free-for-web-search.html

news publishers can now monitor, in real-time, the vital statistics of individual stories; plotting what is most popular versus what is least popular, and hence which content is most valuable from an advertising and sponsorship viewpoint. Never before has it been possible for publishers to cross-reference readership and advertising sales data with such accuracy.

In practice, the influence of the clickstream is still at a very early stage. For example, news chiefs at both quality and popular media outlets emphasised to us the important division between editorial decisions and commercial imperatives:

> *In all my time here, not once have I been asked [by management], 'We would appreciate you not doing that story because they are big advertisers with us'. Once you go down that road, you lose your credibility.*

> *Marketing have very focused ideas about advertising revenues in and around news slots. That's a completely dark art to me. I don't even know how they target advertising. We have complete editorial independence.*

> *We do not break down revenues by story. We are editorially pure in that sense. I am custodian of journalism; there is no commercial pressure to dilute standards … to place stories just for advertising potential.*

> *A top web story was 'Man gets adopted by squirrel'. Should the journalist who wrote this get paid more than the journalist who brought in the story that could bring down a Home Secretary? You have stories that bring you kudos, stories that bring you clicks, stories that massage the ego of the newspaper. We need them all.*

However, the boundary that protects the purity of editorial decisions from the profit-oriented dynamics of advertising is now under greater pressure than before—because of the precision of the metrics of the clickstream. Never before have editors been able to see with such clarity which stories generate most interest, and thus most improve circulation or ratings. Once publishers convert to a fully integrated method of production, the flow of data from the web will be faster, more detailed and much harder to ignore.

More specifically, there will be considerable pressure on editors and executives to review the popularity and revenue performance of content, the actual value of specific journalists to the brand, as well as the overall efficacy of resource allocation across the organization. Some of our interviewees reported that, at certain quality and tabloid newspapers, year-end journalist salaries are now being negotiated in the light of clickstream data. Even at editorially focused bastions such as the *Guardian*, there is clear anxiety about where the clickstream will lead:

> *There is no collision between editorial values and advertising at the moment, but it is always possible ... The future will certainly be more metric dominated once we integrate ... I am nervous about that future ... Clearly if something is there and no one is reading it, you have to evaluate why you are doing it. But a balance has to be struck. You cannot start firing journalists—who may be a great and important part of our brand—just because they don't bring enough clicks our way. (Alan Rusbridger, Editor, Guardian)*

The clickstream affects the entire spectrum of UK news publishers. Our view is that, in the quest for digital success, news publishers are being nudged insistently to depart from well-established brand and editorial values—in turn, contributing to the development of a softer and more populist news agenda in the UK. Evidence for this trend can be found in two general areas, which we examine in greater detail in Chapter 6. The first is the allocation of web space and resources to coverage that is appetising to web audiences in general, or particular segments of that audience (e.g. the international component). The second is the growing preference for comment and opinion over hard news, which tends to enhance the appeal of news brands to global audiences on the web, not least because 'star commentators' and so-called 'super-journalists' provide a personality—a cultural lens—through which consumers can navigate and digest the news.

The visibility of the clickstream—coupled to wider commercial pressures—provides an accelerant to the so-called 'rat pack' effect, as described by Tony Blair in his Reuters Institute speech about the UK media in June 2007. As he commented, 'The audience needs to be arrested, held and their emotions engaged. Something that is interesting is less powerful than something that makes you angry or shocked.'[77] That phenomenon is arguably intensifying as news publishers huddle under the umbrella of sensationalist and popular stories in a bid to contain costs (in news-

---

[77] http://news.bbc.co.uk/1/hi/uk_politics/6744581.stm

gathering) and boost ratings (across a range of media platforms). For example, a fundamental paradox of the 24/7 media environment is that the news agenda has become more homogeneous—more anchored around high-profile stories—despite a proliferation of channels through which the news can be accessed.[78] Due to the integration of newsrooms, there is clear duplication of stories across print, broadcast, online and other new media channels. As more news consumers migrate online, the clickstream is likely to assume an even more important role in the shaping of the news agenda.

Looking ahead, the clickstream has the capacity not only to transform the nature and breadth of the news agenda—it would also lead news publishers into new and uncharted territory, where well-established brand and editorial values face redefinition. In our view, news publishers are in danger of diluting their brand into a 'digital windsock', which is merely given shape by the prevailing direction of the clickstream. The basic logic of a web-centric strategy is to maximise the size of the audience around the news, for as long as possible. By default, that strategy tends to favour a 'softer' and more populist orientation to the news agenda, given its ability to generate spikes in consumption. Preference is logically given to topics such as celebrity, entertainment and sports, which are viewed as effective generators of traffic.

A vivid example is the increasingly celebrity-oriented feel of the Mail Online, which is steadily drifting into territory that its owners would not consider suitable for printing. As one industry observer predicted,

> *The Daily Mail group will wake up in 10 years with two brands: a showbiz freak show online, and a relatively conservative product in print, which can afford to take the moral high ground on various issues thanks to the appeal of its sensationalist approach to life in general.*

The distant and relatively ill-defined promise of the clickstream is also luring quality daily newspapers into a more populist, comment-driven and tabloid-like style, which is designed to attract eyeballs from the international ether of the web. For example, the inclusion of entirely new categories of coverage—such as 'celebrity', 'lifestyle' and 'weird'—to the websites of the *Daily Telegraph*, *The Times* and the *Guardian* underscores the radical difference between these newspapers and their pre-digital counterparts.

---

[78] Relatively speaking: news publishers are also seeking to find ways of differentiating themselves; see Ch. 6 on changes to newsgathering.

The populist slant of ITV News is also illustrative. Mark Wood (CEO of ITN) admitted that there are serious challenges to covering the hard news topics of the day in a fashion that is appetising to the mainstream audience. The potential result is a distorted 'echo chamber', which simply reflects and reinforces the mass interests of the crowd. Mark Wood is aware of the dangers:

> *We are certainly doing a lot more coverage of show biz and entertainment … The huge risk with demand-led news is that people will just look at a fraction of what is actually going on in the world; the tiny segment that interests them … the whole world can be collapsing around you but you wouldn't know.*

The lure of the clickstream—and the attendant popularization of the news agenda—therefore raises a series of critical social and civic questions, linked to the role of the media as a source of information in democratic decision-making, which we explore further in Chapters 7 and 8. The changes underway also raise questions about the future shape and relevance of news brands. For example, a rush to generate clicks may in fact erode the distinctiveness of the brand and its connection to a specific audience. By anchoring their brand identities in softer content, news publishers risk losing traffic (to specialised sites that provide show business and sports news more effectively) and advertisers (who are increasingly demanding engaged not transitory eyeballs, especially in the quest to build brand awareness).

A more viable strategy, we suggest, is for news publishers to identify and follow 'editorial isolines' as they navigate the trails of the clickstream. In practice, that would entail a strategic focus on certain kinds of coverage and hence, certain audiences, whilst sidelining others.

The search for digital success would be refracted through the prism of existing editorial and brand values. The purpose would be to focus on the qualitative rather than the quantitative dimensions of web audiences. In other words, the publisher would seek to engage a particular type of audience, rather than focusing on the absolute maximization of eyeballs, which tends to disregard the characteristics and location of audiences. In turn, that might curry favour with advertisers seeking to access that type of audience. Sir Peter Job (former CEO of Reuters) suggests that, with a distinctive audience-focused approach, news publishers would be better able to position themselves within the web of information search and advertising transactions on the web.

A strategic focus of this kind would be challenging, culturally and operationally, given the inexorable race amongst publishers and journalists to outperform each other on the latest web rankings. Grand claims of new web traffic records now abound on a regular basis, reflecting the salience of clickstream performance in the market. Nonetheless, a more targeted focus on audience characteristics—not size or volume alone—would have the potential to sustain a more robust business model over the longer term. For example, the engagement of audiences around targeted and relevant news content is more likely to attract and sustain the interest of advertisers. As Douglas McCabe (Enders Analysis) pointed out, advertisers are increasingly demanding access to well-defined groups of loyal and engaged audiences, not the transitory eyeballs that are briefly attracted by the flicker of salacious or sensationalist stories.

Elements of this strategic approach can be found at the *Guardian*, which enjoys the protection of the wealthy Scott Trust. The Guardian Media Group described its approach in its submission to the House of Lords Select Committee thus:

> *Put simply, The Guardian exists to create public value, not private gain. Its unique ownership structure means that the wider Guardian Media Group does not seek profit for the financial benefit of its owners or shareholders, but to sustain journalism that is free from commercial or political interference, and to uphold a set of values laid down by our former Guardian editor, CP Scott and now enshrined as the Scott Trust values.*[79]

Despite a certain degree of drift into popular realms, the brand remains focused around a core set of principles. Tim Brooks (Managing Director of Guardian News & Media) admits that categories such as 'lifestyle' and 'food' are modern but necessary appendages to the underlying editorial mission of the newspaper. That mission, he suggests, remains firmly rooted in the vision of founder C. P. Scott. The *Guardian* is one of the few UK news publishers to articulate a distinctive set of brand values—encapsulated as 'the world's leading liberal voice'—as it migrates onto the web.

The management team envision the *Guardian* brand acting as a 'digital anchor' within a much broader 'federation' of web content, extending from their own website into the interstices of the blogosphere. Emily Bell (the *Guardian*'s Director of Digital Content) summarises the position:

[79] Guardian Media Group submission to the House of Lords Select Committee (Jan. 2008), 8: www.parliament.uk/documents/upload/Guardian%20Media%20Group%20070208.pdf

We cannot and will not just keep pumping resources into a story to generate clicks. Our approach is to define the Guardian's interest in a story. The question is what angle can we take that is distinctive (e.g. the McCann story) without blindly following the media scrum? In certain cases, the Guardian will make a conscious choice not to be top online. So our search for clicks is constantly being refracted through the liberal prism on the world.

The idea is to aggregate a symbiotic blend of content, audiences and advertising that reflect and buttress the liberal values of the *Guardian* brand. Two examples illustrate this point. The first is the selected identification and enrolment of blogs and partner websites around particular topics, such as the environment. Steve Folwell (Head of Strategy at the Guardian Media Group) explained the team is seeking to create a network of 'like-minded' sites into which *Guardian* content can be syndicated and advertising space sold. The second is the selected use and rejection of advertising around the news. Tim Brooks recounted several instances in which the *Guardian* had declined substantial commercial deals due to clear incompatibilities between the identity of advertisers or sponsors and the message of a given section of the newspaper.

The *Guardian* is not alone. An editorially focused approach to the clickstream is also taking root in premium news publications such as the *Financial Times* or *The Economist*—both of which have close ties to a diversified media owner, Pearson. For these publications, the distinctiveness of their editorial voice is key, perhaps even more so as they expand online and reach new audiences abroad. As Daniel Franklin (Executive Editor) noted, the web has forced *The Economist* team to define and manage the brand and voice in a digital 24/7 format:

The challenge for a weekly [paper] like us is how to stay fresh every day. It's analogous to the Sunday Papers, which have turned to the internet to keep their brands alive during the week. Our strength is addressing the news of the week in a focused, disciplined and space-constrained fashion—e.g. Europe in 5 pages … There's a risk that embracing the internet would erode that discipline. But we have been conscious in our efforts to keep the online offering as tight and focused. Online is still a curated selection which complements our print product.

The strategic vision of the brand—and the relative importance of editorial versus commercial imperatives in the navigation of the click-stream—has profound implications for patterns of spending on news. Following editorial isolines, for example, means investing in the content and newsgathering capabilities that dovetail with the brand and the editorial voice. For most publishers, that is an expensive proposition. A digital windsock, in contrast, can be fuelled with cheaper content, drawn from the wires, public relations and the audience; although the market value of sensationalist stories does continue to drive an underworld of suspect and well-resourced newsgathering activities, as described by Nick Davies in *Flat Earth News*.

In the years ahead, there is likely to be a growing rift between the 'value chains' of publishers that pursue these alternative routes: digital anchor versus digital windsock. As we next describe in Chapter 6, there is a generalised pressure to focus on the processing as opposed to the generation of content. To cut costs, news publishers are looking for ways to boost productivity and enhance efficiencies. The few publishers that do have the luxury of cross-subsidy will become havens for newsgathering (albeit in a streamlined form) against a backdrop of cutbacks and efficiency-driven integration.

6.   The news value chain

As the digital revolution gathers pace, news publishers are beginning to re-evaluate the resources (staff, technology, capital) they allocate across the *value chain*—that is, the various operational phases through which news content is gathered, processed and eventually distributed to the consumer (see Table 6.1).[80] It is difficult to know, with any precision, exactly how spending in the value chain is shifting, due to the immense secrecy that surrounds the fiscal structure of media owners, as well as the relatively nascent state of digital integration.

Stage	Generation	Processing	Distribution
Activities	**Internal:** - Desk research - Permanent bureaux - Mobile stringers	**Preparation:** - Filtering stories - Packaging content - Verification	**Multi-Channel Delivery:** - Print/broadcast - Web - Mobile
	External: - Wire agencies - Public relations - Citizen journalism	**Digital Versioning:** - Multimedia content - SEO techniques - Semantic enrichment	**Interactivity:** - Managing dialogue - Tracking performance - Clickstream analysis
Key Trends	- Contraction of bureaux - Flexible use of resources - Increased use of external material	- Integration of newsroom operation - Investment in IT systems - De-layering and cost savings	- Culture of metrics - Exposure of journalists to multiple channels - Emphasis on dexterity and generalism

Table 6.1. Components of the twenty-first-century news value chain

---

[80] In practice, these phases overlap; for example, technology enables journalist to simultaneously gather and process information from their desks in the newsroom.

However, we are able to outline the emerging directions of change in the news value chain. As Table 6.1 suggests, there is a series of overlapping and sometimes contradictory trends, reflecting patterns of investment as well as retrenchment. A common theme is the inexorable lure of integration. Across the industry, news value chains are becoming anchored in some form of digital hub. The success of the integrated newsroom depends on a distinctive matrix of assets—multi-skilled journalists, expensive technology platforms—that can efficiently convert multiple information feeds into a marketable portfolio of web content. As we show in this chapter, this has profound implications for the craft of professional journalism.

At one end of the value chain, news publishers require far more content than they can deliver alone. To feed the appetite of 24/7 media platforms, news publishers are increasingly reliant on a range of external suppliers for the raw material of journalism: not only trusted wire agencies, but also the public relations industry and, more recently, citizen journalism. At the other end of the value chain, news publishers are searching for new journalistic skills to make their content as relevant and sticky as possible within the hyperlinked maze of the web—via clickstream analysis, search engine optimization, embedding of metadata, and new modes of narrative presentation (e.g. wikis and mapping applications).

The overall implication, which underpins this chapter, is that journalists are required to allocate more time to outputs rather than inputs. The digital vision favours skills such as multi-channel dexterity, and enshrines new metrics such as clickstream performance. This is especially the case in digital windsocks, which are focused on the processing and packaging of content, as opposed to the sustained gathering, checking and creation of original content. As a result, the majority of news publishers are cutting back the resources allocated to bureaux and newsgathering, both at home and abroad. The exception is that some digital anchors are increasing their investment in the front line, as a result of cost savings in the newsroom. Publishers of all kinds, however, are searching for more cost-efficient, flexibly organised models of newsgathering, which require journalists to embrace a new form of lightweight but high-pressure working.

To be sure, these changes are delivering considerable performance enhancements to the practical work of journalists. Identifying, preparing and writing stories is now easier and faster thanks to the possibilities of the web: in particular, research, once a comparatively time-consuming business of tracking down sources and documents, is hugely assisted by powerful search engines and the libraries of material now on the web. But these changes also herald fundamental changes in the life of the journalist.

There is a danger, in particular, that journalists will become 'prisoners of the screen': cogs in a digitally mechanised and highly demanding news factory, which erodes the time available for original reporting, reflection and analysis. The paradox of integration, therefore, is that it creates a series of hidden costs and challenges that potentially limit the ability of journalists—as Tim Brooks noted earlier, it heralds 'complexity rather than simplicity'. The situation is compounded by the differential between the costs and revenues of digital news operations: revenues from the web, for example, are still overshadowed by the fixed and variable costs (e.g. systems installation, digital training, branding) necessary to achieve operational momentum.

Our conclusion, as a result, is that there are remarkably few havens where the resource needs of an integrated news operation—that is, multi-skilled journalists, trained to use the functionality of digital asset management platforms—can be sustained over time. Outside the protective shell of the BBC, those havens are most likely to reside within diversified media groups, which have the capital to support the costs of newsgathering, and the systems, skills and content needed to win on the web. For these media groups, journalism will remain a valuable generator of content, which can be sold across multiple divisions—for example, *FT* journalists publishing books through the Penguin label.

6.1. There is a net contraction in the geographical reach of newsgathering networks, both domestically and internationally

Due to the fragmentation of audiences and the reallocation of advertising, the net revenue generated per journalist is in decline. This downward trend is forcing news publishers to review the resources they allocate to the sourcing and generation of content, both domestically and internationally. The front line of newsgathering is therefore being scaled back: specialist correspondents, foreign bureaux and long-term investigative reports are increasingly a luxury that only a few publishers can afford. As a result, the past few years have witnessed a large-scale cull of foreign staff, across newspapers and broadcasters, both in the UK and abroad.[81]

[81] In a study for Harvard's Shorenstein Centre, Jill Carroll found that between 2002 and 2006 the number of foreign-based correspondents employed by US newspapers declined from 188 to 141, due to the increasingly prohibitive costs of maintaining foreign bureaux. See the report for further details: *Foreign News Coverage: The US Media's Undervalued Asset* (2007), available at:
http://www.hks.harvard.edu/presspol/research_publications/papers/working_papers/2007_1.pdf

Speaking to the House of Lords Select Committee on Communications, Robert Thomson (former Editor of *The Times*), commented: 'The first thing that newspapers do when they are in financial trouble is to close foreign bureaux.'[82] Reflecting this view, David Schlesinger (Editor in Chief at Reuters) told the Committee that it is a 'world wide fact that newspapers are cutting back on foreign correspondents and using more agency feed'. As one editor remarked to us, commercial pressures and technological possibilities increasingly favour a shift in focus from the generation to the processing of content:

> *Think of news production as a spectrum; at one end, you have journalists in tents, gathering stories ... at the other end, there is news processing—what you can do there is make quite a smart looking news programme without actually spending much on journalism. The pressure is clearly to move towards the other end, towards news processing, to lessen your investment in original journalism.*

The huddling effect in the UK news media is a logical response to current pressures. It makes economic sense to funnel scarce resources into the coverage of *tent-pole* stories that can be relied upon to attract a stream of eyeballs both to websites and print or broadcast channels.[83] This makes even more sense considering it is now possible (thanks to the detail of the clickstream) to accurately correlate traffic spikes with particular kinds of coverage. A broadcast news chief described to us the 'powerful buzz' that is now created in his newsroom when a story explodes online:

> *The breaking news of Shannon Matthews being alive is an example. We were just watching the clicks go up like a petrol pump on the ... website. In the course of an hour we had 60,000 hits!*

Thus, the clickstream is likely to cement the centripetal tendencies of the news media, making the refuge of sensationalist and populist stories even more enticing. The so-called 'rat pack' effect serves to artificially narrow the news agenda and thereby contain the underlying costs of newsgathering. The huddling of the news media is self-reinforcing: having directed resources to a particular story or location, it makes sense to maximise that coverage for as long as possible, before switching to the next tent-pole story.

---

[82] House of Lords Select Committee on Communications, *The Ownership of the News,* vol. 1, *Report* (2008), 19.

[83] Recent examples in the UK include the disappearance of Madeleine McCann or Shannon Matthews, or the death of Christopher Foster and family in August 2008.

Content analysis appears to support this general dynamic. For example, research by Professor James Curran (Goldsmiths, University of London) has found that the UK news media are shifting towards the softer, entertainment-oriented model of the US, and away from the harder, factually oriented model of public service havens such as Denmark and Finland. A more recent longitudinal study of UK television (comprising news and other programming) reached a similar conclusion:

> *As increasing globalization and migration require us to interact with other cultures and our economic, political and social inter-dependence with other countries becomes ever more apparent, so there is a growing need for UK citizens to have a greater awareness and understanding of the wider world and their place in it. As UK citizens' primary source of information about the wider world, television is uniquely placed to inform and educate audiences about other places ... The results of this study show that the international factual output of the four main terrestrial channels in 2007 was the lowest recorded since these reports began ... The data highlights the increasing migration of international factual content to digital channels, which now make up 24 per cent of the total, the highest figure to date. 'Soft' programming topics such as travel continue to dominate whilst 'harder' ones such as conflict and disaster and politics constitute only 12 per cent of all inter-national factual output.*[84]

The economic dynamics of the contemporary UK media increasingly favour soft versus hard news, notably in broadcast but also in print. The decision by executives at the BBC and commercial publishers alike to invest in activities such as celebrity and entertainment news—even as they cut back foreign coverage and reduce the fees awarded to their worldwide network of freelancers—underscores the industry-wide belief that soft news is the key to engaging the younger generation of audiences.

Despite its softening tone, the UK news agenda continues to be shaped by powerful competitive undercurrents. Even within the established paradigm of 'group think', news publishers continue to seek content—through their own newsgathering activities, or from external suppliers—that will strengthen or differentiate their brand in some fashion. In fact, the level of competition between publishers is arguably intensifying due to the scarcity of digital audiences and the potential value of original, breaking

---

[84] http://www.dfid.gov.uk/pubs/files/screeningreport-020608.pdf

stories across multiple platforms. The permanence of digital content—and the chance to reach global audiences—provides a powerful incentive for journalists to break a new story or find an original angle. The imperative for news publishers, therefore, is to find ways of cutting the cost of news-gathering, whilst remaining productive and competitive.

6.2. As they restructure, news publishers are searching for more agile, flexible and cost-efficient models of newsgathering

Whether the aforementioned cuts to newsgathering are actually impairing the breadth and quality of journalism—and hence, its civic function—is a subject of fierce debate, which we examine further in Chapter 7. Here, we simply draw attention to the changing models of newsgathering.

In response to economic pressures, publishers are adopting a more *flexible structure* of newsgathering. Driving that process of restructuring is a wide-spread view that bureaux need to be consolidated around a handful of key hubs, located in regions of strategic, geopolitical and economic importance. That is crucial, given the considerable fixed and variable costs of foreign bureaux. In a recent study for Harvard's Shorenstein Centre, for example, Jill Carroll estimated that a single newspaper foreign bureau costs between $200,000 and $300,000 per year; a figure that is substantially higher in conflict zones due to the cost of logistics and security.

At the forefront of consolidation is ITN, which has more than halved the number of permanent bureaux and staff since 2000. ITN now allocates just 5 per cent of its overall news budget to a network of six foreign bureaux. As Mark Wood explained, ITN has had to prioritise 'mobility over fixity' due to the growing disparity between costs and revenues. There has been increased use of air travel to deploy correspondents to events and locations 'just in time'; moreover, those correspondents tend to be equipped with a toolkit of digital communications technologies which drastically reduce the cost of capturing, editing and transmitting news stories (see below). In parallel, there has been increased use of *stringers* (freelance correspondents, photographers and videographers) worldwide. A broadcast news chief made the following comment:

> *The old fashioned, big bureaux with the producer, the correspondent, the camera crew, technicians, etc., are increasingly looking inefficient. People are now looking at more flexible, mobile staffing—so having*

journalists that can shoot, edit and report on the go. For example, part of the money I got in the new budget is for hiring 'super-fixers'; people who will be based around the world, not in a bureaux, on a retainer contract, and will be the first line of response in the event of a big story. So it's a shift away from bricks and mortar towards roving reporters.

Under pressure to cut costs in light of the revised licence fee, the BBC has also had to restructure its newsgathering operations. Over the next five years, for example, 100 out of 700 newsgathering posts will be removed as the BBC consolidates its bureaux structure around a handful of strategic hubs. That process has sparked conflict with permanent staff and free-lancers, not least because of ongoing inflation in the wages of star celebrities, commentators and news anchors.

Nonetheless, there is a clear disparity between the newsgathering operations of the BBC and its commercial rivals. Lacking the shelter of public subsidy, ITN and Sky have had to streamline their operations and adopt a model of flexible production, which is designed to aggregate and reversion content for a range of media platforms and clients. Peter Phillips (Partner in Strategy and Market Developments at Ofcom) explained that the defining characteristic of commercial broadcast news production is the 'reliance on pooled material', both internally generated and externally sourced (through the wires and beyond).[85] To be sure, elements of this approach can also be detected at the BBC (see below); but the model is especially pronounced in the commercial sector, where, as noted, diminishing revenues and profits are forcing publishers to cut back spending and extract the maximum value from their existing resources.[86]

ITN, for example, draws content from its entire newsgathering network and external feeds when producing and customising news packages for clients such as ITV, Channel 4, the Independent Radio Network, and more recently, Telegraph TV. It also reversions content, at minimal cost, for new markets such as mobile news (distributed to subscribers of Vodafone and other network providers). In a similar fashion, Channel 5 news is able to piggyback on the newsgathering resources of Sky News, where it is produced.

Newsgathering in the commercial broadcast news sector is therefore dependent upon a distinctive pooling and sharing of resources. The news-gathering capabilities of the wire agencies perform a comparable function, both for print and broadcast. In a context of resource constraint, it is

[85] House of Lords Select Committee on Communications, '*The Ownership of the News,* vol. 1, *Report* (2008), 25.
[86] http://www.ft.com/cms/s/0/88359750-b76e-11dd-8e01-0000779fd18c.html

simply impossible for news publishers to remain proximate to events as they unfold. As we noted earlier, that is increasing the dependence of publishers on the wire agencies, in addition to the public relations industry and the emerging army of 'citizen journalists' (both of which now supply torrents of free news content on a daily basis).

This general backdrop is complicated, however, by scattered evidence of increased investments in newsgathering. Amidst the wider commercial landscape of streamlining and flexibility, for example, there are distinct pockets—typically around digital anchors rather than windsocks—in which certain elements of newsgathering are being expanded not retrenched.

The strategic orientation and operational structure of certain news publishers has enabled the reallocation of resources into newsgathering, particularly in the area of foreign coverage. In particular, cost savings brought about by the integration of news processing (see above) have in some cases freed resources, which can be diverted into coverage budgets. Guy Ker (Chief Operating Officer of ITN) even suggests that efficiencies are bringing down the overall cost of broadcast news production. As he argues, flexible budgets are now a source of competitive differentiation—separating out those publishers that can quickly switch gears between different stories and locations:

> *It's just as well costs are coming down, because the requirement to have flexible budgets that can be used to cover any news eventuality, from going live from melting icecaps to purchasing the latest schlock-horror video of a jailed LA temptress, has never been greater. The breadth of what constitutes news is wider than it has ever been.*

According to our research, the overall proportion of the ITN news budget allocated to newsgathering has increased by 15 per cent over the past 10 years, thanks in large part to the realization of cost efficiencies in the news-room. Following the integration of ITN's newsroom, for example, both ITV and Channel 4 decided to allocate additional funds to foreign news coverage. Channel 4 alone increased its coverage budget by 20 per cent in 2008; in particular, to enable its distinctive brand of 'special reports' and 'live debates', shot in foreign locations such as Israel, Iran and China. In addition, the cost savings achieved by ITN in news processing have enabled Channel 4 to direct extra resources to the Independents Fund, which is used to orchestrate and finance novel programming and investigative reports. As Jim Gray (Editor of Channel 4 News) describes:

> *The Independents Fund has grown substantially. When I arrived, it was only around £250,000 … in the recent contract negotiation it jumped to £1.5m. We are able to do that kind of investment because of broader synergies and technological advances at Ch4 news. I can afford to do this; not by cutting back elsewhere in our coverage, but by being more efficient with our resources. It's a balance; we try to cover the core news, but also add independent content to the mix. What the Fund has pioneered is to help set up new companies and production entities … Guaranteed income from the Fund means that the production team can employ a researcher, have certainty in their project. This is vital because investigative reporting is onerous and expensive with a high failure rate.*

In the print sector, there is also scattered evidence that cost savings are helping to expand areas of newsgathering. According to Tim Brooks, the Guardian Media Group has increased its editorial budget every year since 2003; the number of full-time editorial staff has grown from 438 in 2004 to 465 in 2008 on the *Guardian*, and from 145 to 162 on the *Observer* over the same time frame.[87] And due to its digital success, the *Guardian* has increased its base of foreign correspondents in the USA from 5 to 12 over the past two years, in order to better produce content for that market. The integration of the newsroom, from October 2008, is critical to this process of investment. Significantly, in an effort to build on its US success, the *Daily Mail* is planning to launch a New York print edition, which will require extra investments in foreign correspondents.

The *Financial Times* is embarking upon a similar process of foreign expansion, notably in Asia, where it is attracting a growing number of web users. The provision of accurate and up-to-date coverage of foreign events is increasingly appealing to consumers in the context of the wider financial crisis. In September 2008, for example, FT.com experienced a 250 per cent surge in unique web users in the immediate aftermath of the collapse of AIG, Lehman Brothers and Merrill Lynch—in addition to a 20 per cent boost in print circulation.[88] There is clear demand for trusted coverage of

---

[87] The growth is actually understated as the Guardian Media Group included web developers in the editorial headcount in 2004 but now counts them separately.
[88] http://www.journalism.co.uk/2/articles/532382.php

global economic and political issues. As Kate Koch (CFO of FT Group) explained, 'general news is a commodity; but business analysis is a premium product that not many can do on a global basis'. Developments at the *Guardian* and the *Financial Times* suggest that digital growth may provide the economic foundations on which some form of permanent foreign coverage can continue to survive.

The premium brand value that accrues from specialist foreign coverage has spurred some news publishers to find more cost-efficient ways of retaining (or even expanding) a front-line presence. That can be achieved through 'just in time' deployments of correspondents, or through the employment of freelance stringers.

Simon Jenkins remarked to us that in any given 'theatre of war', there are now far more correspondents on location—with many despatched from quality daily newspapers such as the *Guardian* or *The Times*—than there were during previous conflicts, such as Afghanistan or Suez. In the current geopolitical context, moreover, it is virtually impossible to accurately cover mainstream stories without detailed knowledge of developments at an inter-regional and international scale. A handful of news publishers see the provision of foreign coverage as an essential component of their product and broader civic function. As Robert Thomson (former Editor of *The Times*) has suggested, excessive cuts to newsgathering will result in the

> the global diversity of British newspaper coverage [being] diminished … The specialist, whether it is political or business specialist, whether it is the lay reporter, whether it is the home affairs reporter, is an absolutely essential translator of issues in British society for a broader audience. The ideal specialist is very familiar with evolving debate, can point out to a reader who trusts that person when there is an issue that they should be concerned about and why that development is meaningful … So, the specialist journalists at *The Times* and other newspapers I would argue are national leading treasures.[89]

A final caveat relates to the issue of cross-subsidy. At some news publishers, journalists and correspondents are given the latitude to specialise in a particular area, and subsequently produce book-length

---

[89] House of Lords Select Committee on Communications, *The Ownership of the News,* vol. 1, *Report* (2008), 19.

analyses of topics and events. In effect, these kinds of books represent a form of investigative reporting and thereby make a valuable contribution to the dynamism of the wider news media.

Entry into the book trade is generally advantageous both for the personal brand of the journalist and the corporate brand of the media publisher for which they write; indeed, the book may even be published through a sister division of a media group. To varying degrees, publishers such as the *Guardian*, *The Times*, the *Financial Times* and *The Economist* offer their journalists a culture that encourages and supports the writing of books. The basic point is that news publishers are contributing to the dynamism of the UK book trade, which provides those publishers with an additional welcome stream of revenue, and in turn they are enabling more distributed, prolonged forms of newsgathering to continue. Again, this shows that professional newsgathering is changing shape, not disappearing entirely.

6.3. Web technologies are radically expanding the scope of newsgathering and the investigative capabilities of journalists

As news publishers restructure and streamline their front-line operations, they are equipping correspondents and journalists with an arsenal of computing and communications devices. The underlying goal is to enhance the productivity and performance of newsgathering. The era of the fixed bureau is therefore giving way to a more lightweight, mobile form of journalism—in which news content can be recorded, edited and delivered from any location with an internet connection.

Armed with a GPS-enabled phone, laptop, mobile broadband and digital video recorder, the modern journalist is able to perform a startling range of duties in the field. The latest generation of web applications— search, maps, social networks –enable journalists to prepare and triangulate material for a story en route to an event or location. A common misconception is that the digital revolution is leaving the professional journalist redundant in a sea of blogs and citizen journalists. In reality, the technological possibilities of the digital revolution are empowering and extending the craft of journalism in ways that were unimagined just a few years ago.

However, the technological transformation of journalism is fundamentally driven by economic considerations. News publishers are investing in digital technologies in order to reduce the overall cost of the value chain. For example, the digitally armed journalist is increasingly a generalist rather than a specialist, who is expected to provide a range of content for multiple platforms:

> *The journalist of the future will be able to shoot pictures, write for online, have a broadcasting voice in radio and television, and will be self-starting. That's how a correspondent will get themselves on the rung. (Fran Unsworth, Head of BBC Newsgathering)*

The job specification of journalists is therefore diversifying: the implication is that journalists are being required to assume duties that were hitherto performed by other specialists, for example in the newsroom itself. The overall trend is towards the deployment of autonomous roving journalists— as Mark Wood (CEO of ITN) puts it: 'the single operator cameraman', who can independently record, edit and submit news stories. The internet is now an integral channel of communication between journalists and the newsroom, particularly for breaking news stories demanding live coverage.

By using the internet, news publishers can obviate the need for expensive satellite transmissions. Due to ongoing advances in broadband speeds and video compression technology, news publishers are now able to source broadcast-quality images direct from digitally equipped journalists. For example, the BBC has recently launched a new application that enables correspondents to directly upload video from a mobile device to the broadcast server—from where content is processed and fed to the television news and the bbc.co.uk website.

Sky News, meanwhile, is now using a managed internet delivery network (trialled during coverage of the Iraq war in 2007), which can compress and transmit high-quality broadcast images from correspondents. Although bandwidth intensive, the overall cost of internet-based delivery is cheaper than satellite transmissions. Bevan Gibson (Head of Future Technology, Sky News) estimates that the elimination of satellite connections—and the shipping of heavy broadcast equipment—is resulting in cost savings of up to £1,500 per hour of broadcasting time.[90] In a similar vein, Guy Ker (Chief Operating Officer of ITN) predicts that

---

[90] http://www.computing.co.uk/computing/news/2188590/sky-news-starts-ip-broadcasts

the next big quantum reduction in costs [will come] from easier delivery of picture: all the infrastructure associated with satellite picture delivery: satellite paths, technical coordinators, SNG vehicles, Master Control centres ... are likely to reduce as file-based picture transfer takes hold and becomes common place and easy.[91]

Despite its capacity to enhance newsgathering, however, the deployment of digital technology also has serious drawbacks. The new agility of flexible newsgathering is also matched by a new fragility, which threatens the breadth, depth and accuracy of news coverage. The following points can be made.

The growing preference for mobile journalists versus permanently staffed bureaux is likely to lead to a narrowing of reporting and analysis, especially in the area of international news. Writing for the Institute of Communications Studies, University of Leeds, Fred Hiatt (an editor with the *Washington Post*) explains that traditionally

foreign bureaux allowed for a depth and variety of reporting, analysis and interpretation beyond what wire services and foreign media provide. Foreign bureaux helped newspapers attract talented reporters, who in turn returned to their home newsrooms with a sense of the world that worked to readers' benefit.[92]

Reflecting these concerns, Pamela Constable (also at the *Washington Post*, as a foreign correspondent) suggests that mobile journalists will, by default, be less embedded in the social and cultural milieux of foreign contexts:

In an effort to cut costs, newspapers are replacing bureaux—which require staffs and cars and family housing—with mobile, trouble-shooting individual correspondents. The erstwhile bureau chief in New Delhi or Cairo, chatting with diplomats over rum punches on the veranda, is now an eager kid with a laptop and an Arabic phrase book in their backpack.[93]

---

[91] Quoted in Beckett, *Super-Media*.
[92] http://ics.leeds.ac.uk/papers/vp01.cfm?outfit=pmt&folder=193&paper=2770
[93] http://www.pressgazette.co.uk/story.asp?sectioncode=7&storycode=41628&c=1

6.4. The digital arms race engenders a slavish dependence on technology, which valorises speed over contemplation and reflection

Mobilised by their collective digital vision, news publishers are now engaged in a technological arms race, which views the latest gizmos—from mobile phones to digital asset management systems—as an assured route to cost savings, operational de-layering and productivity gains. Illustrating this approach, Paul Cheesbrough (Chief Information Officer at the Telegraph Media Group) recently told delegates at the World Association of Newspaper Conference that the mobile phone would be the next 'killer app' in professional newsgathering, enabling journalists to collect and return content back to 'home base' faster and more cheaply than in the past.[94]

The pace of the arms race, however, is cementing a new kind of technological dependency, which is in danger of transforming journalists into 'prisoners of the screen'. As newsgathering is scaled back, many journalists begin and finish a story entirely in the office—most likely via a search engine such as Google—without any face-to-face contact with the individuals and organizations that shape the meaning and significance of a particular event or story. That necessarily increases their reliance on external suppliers such as PR agents. In a growing number of cases, moreover, NGOs are funding visits and trips by journalists to particular events or locations—but with little if any transparency about their involvement.

Even for the lucky journalists that do venture beyond the office, meanwhile, the task of newsgathering is increasingly mediated and dictated by an array of devices, all clamouring for attention and ever-faster feedback. The integration of IT systems in the latest newsrooms exposes journalists to the gaze of surveillance, as their performance is quantified and tracked in real-time. In general, journalists are under growing pressure to use digital technology to make their news reports 'slicker, snappier and snazzier, particularly for the web' (as described by Shelby Coffey, a former Editor of the *LA Times*). As a broadcast news chief noted:

> *If you look at programmes 10 years ago, what you notice is that our news programmes are now much faster paced—we pack a lot more in, they are better produced ... Everyone has had to get better at slicing, dicing and packaging news, most of all to keep people's attention.*

[94] http://www.guardian.co.uk/media/greenslade/2008/jun/03/wan2008mobilewillbeaspop

The collateral damage of the digital revolution is therefore the attention of the journalist. Due to the digital integration of newsrooms, journalists are under growing pressure to meet the demands and productivity targets of multiple channels—namely, broadcast, print, online, mobile. At the *Financial Times*, for example, Hugh Carnegy (Executive Editor) estimates that technological integration has boosted productivity by 10 per cent in the past two years.

That pressure tends to be accentuated by the open-plan, radial design of the integrated newsroom environment, which revolves around a kind of 'Panopticon'—the watchful eye of the central editorial desk. In a throwaway but telling remark during our tour of a recently upgraded television newsroom, a senior executive suggested that 'the new design purposefully makes it much easier to identify slackers'. It is only a slight exaggeration to suggest that journalists are now cogs in a digitally mechanised and highly demanding news factory, in which the productivity of individual components can be monitored and reduced to the simplicity of binary code. The cold, impersonal calculation offered by this quasi-Taylorist scientific management is likely to become more pervasive as news publishers—under serious pressure to cut costs—seek to identify and shed areas of inefficiency.

In a recent survey by the National Union of Journalists, for example, 75 per cent of respondents felt that integration had led to increased work-loads and had reduced the quality of their output; 64 per cent reported that they had been asked to supply material for new platforms without additional resources; and 40 per cent were producing content for new media without any training. In the majority of cases, journalists are being forced to assume new responsibilities without extra compensation or negotiation. In only 22 per cent of the NUJ's constituent chapels were journalists awarded pay increases for added multimedia working. For the majority of journalists, therefore, the advent of multimedia working translates into a pay cut: added responsibilities and longer working hours, but at the same level of compensation. In the accompanying report, the NUJ warns:

> *New media working threatens to be a licence for unscrupulous companies to flog their journalists for extra skills and longer working days without any extra pay. Few companies seem to have matched the expansion of their online operations by recruiting extra staff to satisfy the raging appetite for new media output—this despite the fact that much of it, such as podcasting and videocasting, is more time consuming to package and deliver.*[95]

[95] NUJ *Commission on Multimedia Working* (Dec, 2007), 14: http://www.nuj.org.uk/innerPagenuj.html?docid=605

In most publishers, the situation is compounded by the fixed or contracting size of the resource base available for training, which is typically only 1–3 per cent of revenues. As we suggested in Chapter 5, news publishers are in danger of building digital newsrooms that they cannot afford to fully tool or maintain due to the relentless development and obsolescence of technologies. Commenting on the challenges of digital integration at ITV, a senior executive noted:

> *Our new newsroom is sophisticated, streamlined, has very high standards—there is not that much room for inexperienced trainees. Our options are limited, as the training budget has just been cut again. We have had to save on training to enable us to free up resources to do our main job.*

Implementing a comprehensive training regime, to constantly renew the skills of the digital journalist, is beyond the reach of most publishers. The practical implication is that journalists will lack the full suite of skills necessary to perform in the multimedia environment. In turn, that may increase the incidence of mistakes and errors in news coverage, depending upon the orientation of the publisher and safeguards taken by the editorial team:

> *A smaller number of journalists are under greater pressure to deliver more content, in more formats for more platforms, more pages ... the end result is that despite the best efforts of editors and journalists quality journalism is being compromised. (Jeremy Dear, General Secretary, NUJ)*

A vivid illustration of the dangers of multimedia working can be found at the *Daily Express*, where proprietor Richard Desmond is removing sub-editors in a bid to drastically cut newsroom costs, forcing journalists to submit their stories directly into print and online. That could easily lead to a spate of factual errors and, worse, damaging libel claims against the newspaper. Jeremy Dear suggests that, in fact, the erosion of sub-editing is wider than many assume; and that at many publishers the scope and capability of pre-publication fact-checking are in net decline.

The twenty-first-century newsroom is increasingly a place of digital mechanization, where journalists are bombarded with news feeds, saddled with a wider range of responsibilities, and as a result have less time for the in-depth gathering and checking of material, as well as the quiet contemplation and reflection that can help to differentiate a story. For example, multimedia working portends an erosion of *thinking time*, which is seen to be a critical element of quality journalism:

> *Thinking time is incredibly important to our editorial quality ... not least to ensure that the final piece, whether it is live or packaged, has a sense of context and a depth of understanding. That adds real value to the news, and is especially important for a public service organization ... Our concern is that we avoid the unreflective journalism that continuous rolling news can encourage.* (Peter Horrocks, Head of the BBC Newsroom)

Further interviews at the BBC underscored this threat. To some extent, BBC journalists are experienced in juggling the demands of two channels—television and radio—but as another BBC executive observed, the addition of 24/7 coverage in broadcast and online has dramatically accentuated the well-established trade-off between speed and quality—despite the BBC's enviable resource base:

> *We are agile enough to get to stories, but often lose focus on the output side. If a story breaks for ITN, they have hours more lead time before they actually have to deliver the product. So they can find out more, follow leads, devote more time to doing something crafted. But we have one correspondent and one cameraman being pulled in multiple different directions—they are asked to deliver for 5Live, the website, BBC worldwide and cut a package for the 6pm news.*

News publishers such as the BBC are also discovering distinct rivalries and tensions between channels. On the one hand, there is an economic incentive for publishers to leverage and duplicate content across multiple platforms. On the other hand, there is also a countervailing tendency towards editorial distinctiveness, which resists such duplication. For example, Mark Damazer (Controller of BBC Radio 4) expressed concerns that the pressure to 'reheat' stories from television (e.g. BBC News at 10) on radio (e.g. *The Today Programme*, Radio 4) inculcates an unnecessary degree of repetition in the day-to-day news agenda. Indeed, a cursory glance at the BBC's news output on a given day will reveal a striking degree of standardization as stories are distilled into a series of recurring sound bites, designed to achieve maximum impact across the various platforms, stretching from the website to the transcript read by television news anchors.

A key challenge arising from the integration of newsrooms is how best to share resources and, in parallel, also preserve the distinctive feel of different news products. For many of our interviewees, tackling that issue will depend to a large extent upon unwritten norms and codes of conduct between editorial teams and journalists. For example, *The Times* and the *Sunday Times* remain separate in print but share a single website, a relationship that has demanded a 'new dialogue between editors' (Anne Spackman, Editor of Times Online). A similar dynamic is visible at broadcasters such as ITN and Sky, where as noted a central pool of resources is shared between several news teams.

Finally, the new pressures of multimedia working—combined with the relatively low levels of pay in journalism (as we described in Chapter 4)—will arguably enhance the appeal of related professions, such as public relations and the trade press, thereby accelerating the 'brain drain' of experienced editors and journalists. However, it is worth noting that the exposure afforded by the web has also enabled seasoned journalists to cement their positions as respected analysts and commentators in the media. The web also enables journalists to sever their connection to single brands; and instead go about building a personal brand that can be fused with multiple media brands. As a result, Tim Toulmin (Director of the Press Complaints Commission) believes that on the whole journalists are

> *energised by the online opportunity, because more people are reading their copy and less of their copy is being wasted ... Material that would have been cut out due to space constraints is ending up online ... From one perspective, that is maximising the value of what they are doing.*

Over time, the accretion of positive web exposure can translate into bonuses, promotions, as well as headhunting. As we noted earlier, journalist salaries at some publishers are now being negotiated in light of their overall contribution to web traffic and advertising. In several instances, moreover, foreign media have poached successful UK journalists, whose profile has been bolstered in part by the shift towards 24/7, multi-channel news coverage. In 2007, for example, *The Times* lost two of its leading Middle Eastern correspondents to the *New York Times* (Stephen Farrell) and *Los*

Angeles Times (Ned Parker). The digital revolution is therefore beginning to lubricate the circulation of talent within the news media:

> *It's interesting to see that our reporters are being hired by international news organizations. It is a reflection of the strength of the online presence of brands such as The Times and the Guardian that our talent is being targeted by groups such as the New York Times and Los Angeles Times and shows that British reporting is widely respected in the US and beyond. (The Times spokesman, quoted by the Guardian)*[96]

6.5. The digital success of publishers will depend upon cultural and operational changes in the processing and distribution of news

The success of the news value chain is increasingly determined by the processing and distribution capabilities of the integrated newsroom. As they embark upon the path to integration, news publishers are realising that they need to cultivate a set of operational assets—oriented around multi-skilled journalists and integrated technology platforms—that can efficiently and quickly convert multiple information feeds into a portfolio of content which is appetising to both audiences and advertisers.[97]

As we have seen, the demands of the 24/7 multi-channel environment mean that news publishers now require more content than they can deliver alone; practically, that means that information from the front line of news-gathering is being supplemented with externally sourced leads, accounts and even pre-packaged stories. However, the pursuit of an integrated news value chain is forcing news publishers to rethink the way in which news is processed and distributed to the audience. A prominent media commentator observed:

> *The [digital revolution] has consumed far more resources than any news publisher ever imagined ... There is a cultural and institutional challenge of redirecting the company in the new environment—namely, how to convey and imbue the new skills that are needed to extend the brand online.*

---

[96] http://www.guardian.co.uk/media/2007/mar/06/pressandpublishing.thetimes
[97] For a related study, see A. E. Zadrayec, *Fight for your Life: Newspapers and Digital Storytelling* (Research Paper, Reuters Institute for the Study of Journalism, Oxford University, 2008).

A key challenge facing news publishers, as they extend their brands and operations to digital platforms, is how best to process and distribute news content in a form that is both visible and appetising to digital audiences.

As we have seen, the future of news publishers depends upon their ability to construct web properties that can consistently engage the attention of audiences and attract the investment of advertisers. Our research suggests that, to succeed, news publishers will need to address the following issues in the processing and distribution of content. The extent to which publishers are able to confront these issues—and explore their commercial potential—will depend to a significant degree upon their respective strategic vision, the availability of resources, and the presence of any cross-subsidy. In all likelihood, the majority of news publishers will be unable to divert sufficient resources into these new areas.

First and foremost, the web demands new approaches to the writing and presentation of news stories. As many interviewees emphasised, the skills that underpin print journalism are not easily transferable to the web, particularly because of the global distribution of digital audiences. As news websites become more popular, with millions of consumers in a spread of different markets and cultures, otherwise simple issues in the production of stories—such as terminology, definitions and contextualization—can suddenly become extremely complex.

To maintain or extend their digital positions in foreign markets, news publishers are realising that they need to adapt their websites to the tastes, habits and language of overseas users. The *Guardian*, for example, is expanding its deployment of US correspondents to better serve readers of *Guardian America*. For some publishers, however, there are synergies rather than differences between markets. The *Financial Times* is illustrative. John Ridding (CEO) believes that the *FT* can effectively serve its foreign readers from a single hub, with only minor geographic customization, given the increasingly global reach of business and financial developments:

> *We do not want to 'editionalise' too much because our audience is international. A banker in New York is interested in the same issues as a banker in Stockholm or Singapore. The front pages in online are tailored a bit to the region but you'll find pretty much all of the articles in the Europe edition in the Asia and US edition.*

The web also opens up entirely new modes of narrative presentation, which publishers are still struggling to understand and address. Alan Rusbridger (Editor of the *Guardian*) believes that 'audiences increasingly want to graze on non-textual forms of news media'. In the future, for example, that might take the form of collaboratively generated news maps (with embedded video, photography, text and geographically sorted public data), or the migration of physical news products (including television broadcasts and even newspapers) into virtual worlds.

In fact, as broadband connections improve, web applications are likely to incorporate a far greater degree of three-dimensional graphics, in areas ranging from e-commerce to social networking. Recognising that potential, Sky News was the first television news broadcaster to build a permanent presence in the virtual world Second Life, which now has over 15 million residents. Second Lifers are able to obtain a free virtual television set, which streams video feeds from Sky News. Sky has also built a replica of its UK newsroom to enable Second Lifers to explore behind the scenes, interact with journalists and even upload their own commentary and video footage (see Figure 6.1).

Figure 6.1. Sky News goes virtual in Second Life

Source: http://www.secondlife.com

So, in the move to integrate newsrooms, and explore the myriad possibilities of the web, journalists are being thrown into a new medium for which they may be ill prepared and with which they are not at all conversant. We have already explained that news publishers lack the training budgets to comprehensively engender and renew the skills required to harness the evolving web. To be sure, the radial design of newsrooms means that support and advice are reasonably close at hand; indeed, publishers such as the BBC and ITN have hired (supposedly on a temporary basis) *conversion producers* and *floorwalkers*, who are responsible for assisting journalists in the transition to multimedia working. Nonetheless, we encountered a widespread belief among editors and journalists that a certain degree of platform focus is actually positive and desirable. By juggling the demands of multiple channels, journalists are less likely to appreciate and address some of the distinctive requirements of the web.

This connects to the second issue—the growing importance of *search engine optimization* to the processing and distribution capabilities of the integrated newsroom. As we saw in Chapter 2, search engines now function as the gatekeepers to the digital audience. That is forcing news publishers to devise techniques to enhance the visibility and prominence of their stories in search engines and other web-based news aggregators, such as Google News or Digg. Those techniques can be distilled into two general categories: algorithmic and social.

The former is premised upon a detailed understanding of the criteria and programming language that underpin the decisions of search engines such as Google. To succeed, news publishers typically need to tweak their headlines or embed suitable keywords and metadata into their content to attract the interest of the 'bots' (web robots) that report back to Google. In their quest to attract the clickstream, news publishers such as the *Daily Mail* and the *Daily Telegraph* have proved especially adept at the algorithmic approach to search engine optimization—indeed, to such an extent that they frequently dominate search results even for stories that other publishers broke to the media.

A recent example was a story, broken by the *Guardian* in the summer of 2008, about Fatah's use of Google Earth to target Israel. Due to editorial oversight, the *Guardian* decided not to tag that particular story with search-friendly keywords such as 'terrorist'. As a result, the *Guardian*'s story was quickly eclipsed by a rehashed and tagged story at the *Daily Telegraph*. Therefore, editorial cultures can clearly restrict the use of search engine optimization. The crucial debate is how far, and in what ways, should editorial principles be used to navigate the clickstream.

The second approach differs in that it requires a more interactive and social approach to the packaging, seeding and distribution of web content. It is equally important to news publishers, and potentially even more effective given the growing popularity of social media websites (e.g. friendship networks such as Facebook) and other collaborative 'web 2.0' applications, especially among the younger generation of consumers. Advances in search technology also suggest that Google's position may face competition from a new breed of open source search engines which are collectively designed and refined by web users (e.g. Wikia). Understanding the dynamics and evolution of social media is vital to the processing capabilities of integrated newsrooms. As recent recruitment activity indicates, news publishers are betting that specialist expertise linked to blogging, online communities, social networking and digital marketing will be essential to the success of their newsrooms.

The *Guardian*, for example, is recruiting experts that can convey to editors and journalists the importance of what is known as *hyper distribution*—that is, an approach that departs from the relative linearity of print and broadcast distribution, and instead views journalism as an interactive and ongoing conversation with the audience. That necessarily entails seeding news into multiple channels and web communities, as well as managing the *afterlife* of a story through community engagement. As Emily Bell (Director of Digital Content, *Guardian*) noted earlier in the report, newspapers have struggled to position themselves') described, a key challenge is imparting to the newsroom staff the distinctive characteristics of web content and the skills needed to maximise its impact within the audience. Integral to hyper distribution, for example, is the embedding of content within a wider context of coverage and analysis. This leads us to the third issue facing newsrooms, which relates to the *semantic enrichment* of web content.

To sustain advertising revenues, news publishers need to devise ways of keeping consumers on their websites for longer, especially as the majority of users enter and leave (typically within a few minutes) via the 'side door' of search results and RSS feeds. A potential approach is to create a richer, more customised user experience, which situates stories within a broader 'semantic' web of contextually relevant content. For example, that could take the form of embedded hyperlinks to audio-visual and textual content on the server, or specific metadata, to assist in the classification, retrieval and combination of stories (by a range of criteria—e.g. people or places).

In addition, analysis of the clickstream would enable content and semantic recommendations to be tailored to the individual consumer.

In this fashion, news publishers could convey to the audience the actual breadth and depth of content that is available in given areas of coverage and analysis. In turn, that could realistically extend the afterlife of a story; as Professor Robert Picard pointed out, the permanence of the web means that news publishers can keep generating traffic and advertising from their portfolio of content long after publication, assuming that archival content is linked appropriately and clearly. Semantic enrichment through the embedding of relevant hyperlinks could be applied to both regular news and longer-form content, such as investigative reports, where there are clear benefits to the display and cross-referencing of archival material.

In theory, a semantically enriched news website could become a self-sustaining engine of clicks, fuelled by the ongoing replenishment of the portfolio. This is the basic logic that underpins the digitization of news archives: publishers view their archives—what Chris Anderson terms 'the long tail'—as a virtually untapped resource, which can be monetised more effectively through web search.[98] Some publishers, including *The Times*, now believe that a comprehensive and semantically enriched news archive could even be used to justify premium subscription services. In general, though, the majority of publishers continue to pursue an open access and advertising-supported model of archiving: as noted above, Google is effectively cross-subsidising the digitization of over 100 news archives in return for a share of future advertising revenues. In doing so, however, it is positioning itself as a potential gatekeeper to the successful management and monetization of this content.

To implement semantic enrichment, news publishers will need to fundamentally redesign much of the processing and distribution of news content—again, with significant cultural and operational ramifications. Culturally, because the insertion of hyperlinks into stories is still an alien concept to most newsrooms. Alan Rusbridger admitted to us that, at the *Guardian* at least, it 'would be a huge shift to get the newsroom staff to regularly think about the linking and metadata aspect of stories'. As Emily Bell (Director of Digital Content, *Guardian*) noted earlier in the report, newspapers have struggled to position themselves for the unique demands of the web because

A certain degree of exclusivity prevails in the print world ... for example keeping big scoops among a small clique ... whereas the

---

[98] C. Anderson, *The Long Tail* (Hyperion, 2006).

web demands a more open and less secretive approach, which can draw on the skills, resources and existing coverage available to the brand. The model needed for online is more analogous to the production model of broadcast.

In operational terms, achieving semantic enrichment is challenging for both newspapers and broadcasters. This is because the actual process of classifying and organising content in a semantic form still requires a considerable degree of human oversight. Due to wider pressures, news publishers are unlikely to allocate any significant investment to this task (or associated training) in the near future. In theory, some of this work could be performed more cheaply and efficiently by commercial providers, or even by the digital audience (e.g. using a form of open source tagging software). Reflecting the potential of that 'crowd-powered' approach, albeit in a political rather than a media context, is the successful video time stamping project launched by MySociety in June 2008, which relies upon users watching clips of parliamentary debate to render the database searchable by keywords and topics.

For cultural and operational reasons, therefore, the semantic enrichment of news content is still a distant panacea for most news publishers. Progress will most likely be made by publishers that reside within a diversified media group which has the motivation and resources to leverage its portfolio of content in a semantic form. Anne Spackman (Editor of Times Online), for example, predicts that diversified media groups such as News International will be attracted by the concept of a *digital free trade area*, in which there would be open linking and cross-referencing of content from divisions across the organization, and potentially with other publishers also. At present, a vast amount of media content remains trapped in autistic silos: similar to other information-based businesses, media owners have struggled to convert and organise their digital assets at an enterprise scale. The emergence of the 'semantic web' has the capacity to unlock that hidden content and make it visible to a far wider audience.

The BBC, for example, believes it can extract more public value from its archive through the wider use of aggregation tools, customization software and semantic enrichment. Significantly, the logic of digital free trade clearly dovetails with the strategic focus of digital anchors, such as the *Guardian* or the *Financial Times*, which are seeking to build a corral or 'federation' of web content around their brands. That approach will depend upon a critical mass of navigable, compelling and effectively linked web content. Summarising the challenge, Jeff Jarvis suggests that news publishers should 'cover what they do best and link to the rest':

> *That's not how newspapers work now. They try to cover everything because they used to have to be all things to all people in their markets ... But in the age of the link, this is clearly inefficient and unnecessary. You can link to the stories that someone else did and to the rest of the world. And if you do that, it allows you to reallocate your dwindling resources to what matters, which in most cases should be local coverage. This changes the dynamic of editorial decisions. Instead of saying, 'we should have that' (and replicating what is already out there) you say, 'what do we do best?' That is, 'what is our unique value?' ... In the re-architecture of news, what needs to happen is that people are driven to the best coverage, not the 87th version of the same coverage.*[99]

In summary, the lure of digital integration is transforming the entire news value chain, and in the process, is redefining what it means to be a journalist. As we now show, these changes also have implications for the civic function of the UK news media.

[99] http://www.buzzmachine.com/2007/02/22/new-rule-cover-what-you-do-best-link-to-the-rest/

7. A democratic deficit?

The news media plays a central civic role in modern democracies: in an ecological sense, news publishers shape the cultural and information environment in which democratic processes unfold. The information that news publishers gather, process and disseminate underpins, to varying degrees, the decisions, fears and perceptions of citizens, including their engagement with government and other public institutions. The news media has a material impact on the direction of public policy, as well as the profile of companies and the confidence of markets. The gaze of the news media also has the effect of holding governments, individuals and organizations to account—or at least to scrutiny. The collective benefits of sustained reporting tend to outstrip any instances of abusive or questionable behaviour by the news media.

For these reasons, the changing economic foundations of the UK news media must also be understood from a social and democratic angle. The digital revolution would appear to empower citizens and strengthen democratic engagement. The proliferation of news, particularly on the web, might be argued to herald a new era of digital plurality in which citizens have unrivalled access to news, analysis and data not only from around the world, but also from across their own regions and neighbourhoods. The web simplifies the aggregation of news—even by postcode—and makes it easier than ever before to communicate directly with publicly elected officials, as the various initiatives of the quasi-news organization MySociety indicate.[100] That said, the digital revolution is also forcing the news media along a path that may erode the scope and efficacy of its collective civic function.

---

[100] http://www.mysociety.org

We are entering an era of media consumption and distribution in which the economic foundations of news publishers are unravelling. It is still unclear how, or indeed whether, professional journalism—at least on the scale that the UK and other markets have historically enjoyed—will be sustained in the future. Despite some pockets of expansion, there is a net contraction in the reach and capabilities of newsgathering across the regions of the UK and also internationally. In a bid to cut costs, news publishers are consolidating their bureaux and betting that technology— combined with multi-skilled journalists, and extended working hours— can enable a smaller workforce to produce content for a wider range of media platforms. That change has a direct social cost in terms of the breadth and quality of journalism—for example, how publishers cover political debates or how they package news for the audience.

The purpose of this chapter is to set out some key aspects of the collective civic function of the news media, and to consider how that function might be impacted by the digital revolution. In our view, the strategic and operational responses of news publishers (as outlined in Chapters 5 and 6) indicate that the market is moving in directions that may expose elements of a *democratic deficit*. To be sure, we recognise that it might be dangerous to apply an outdated Reithian ontology to the contemporary news media: as Daniel Franklin (Executive Editor of *The Economist*) pointed out,

> *questions of a democratic deficit may be too elitist; we are moving away from traditional conceptions of authoritative media towards something that is larger, more fragmented, more dispersed.*

Nonetheless, we believe that it is vital to consider the path that news publishers are now traversing—and moreover, to clearly and dispassionately evaluate the democratic potholes that may litter that path in the near future. We begin by venturing into the long-running debate about the *quality* of the news—namely, its accuracy and depth. We then consider the impact of sensationalist reporting on the coverage of political debates— a critical link that connects voters with government—and the wider social risks associated with media distortion.

7.1. The collateral damage of the digital revolution is the reduced attention of journalists, and as a result, the 'quality' of the news agenda

Since the arrival of the printing press, there has always been a certain degree of asymmetry between the reality of newsworthy events and the manner in which they are portrayed in the media. That asymmetry derives from the fundamental time constraints facing journalists, the cultures and vested interests of newsrooms, as well as the deep-seated professional and organizational rivalries that strengthen the imperative for speed in the breaking of news stories. The content of the news—its accuracy, its depth and breadth—is therefore contingent and never assured.

In a powerful speech about the corporate social responsibility of the news media, Alan Rusbridger emphasised that journalism has always been an 'exercise in imperfection'.[101] Reflecting this sentiment, David Broder (a Pulitzer prize-winning journalist, now at the *Washington Post*) famously wrote in 1981:

> *I would like to see us say over and over until the point has been made ... that the newspaper that drops on your doorstep is a partial, hasty, incomplete, inevitably somewhat flawed and inaccurate rendering of some of the things we heard about in the past 24 hours ... distorted despite our best efforts to eliminate gross bias by the very process of compression that makes it possible for you ... to read it in about an hour... If we labelled the paper accurately then we would immediately add: But it's the best we could do under the circumstances, and we will be back tomorrow with a corrected updated version ...*[102]

The point, therefore, is that there has never been a *golden age*—journalism has always been characterised by a distinct tension between speed and accuracy, which predates the current digital revolution by a long margin. 'Fundamentally, journalists have always been busy', as John Ridding (CEO of the *FT*) noted.

The emergence of television, and with it a new era of rolling news, sparked concerns about the erosion of journalistic *thinking time* as far back as the 1970s and 1980s. That historical context has been instrumental in

---

[101] http://www.guardian.co.uk/values/socialaudit/story/0,,1926199,00.html
[102] D. S. Broder, *Behind the Front Page: A Candid Look at How the News is Made* (Simon & Schuster, 1981).

the development of systems and editorial guidelines designed to distribute workloads among journalists:

> *Are we asking [the journalists] to do too much? ... All of this has been around for some time ... there's a lot of on the ground experience, which is deep inside the marrow of the people who make these decisions and therefore have a good feel for where over-stretch begins. (Mark Damazer, Controller, BBC Radio 4)*

As Simon Jenkins remarked to us, the overall quality of the British press remains very high, despite wider cost pressures and increases in the speed and latitude of distribution. It is instructive to note, for example, that the integration of newsrooms—and the associated spike in workloads—has not (as yet) resulted in an implosion of journalism. Echoing the views of other news chiefs, a senior broadcast executive emphasised the strategic importance of flexibility in the newsroom operation:

> *We just have to be flexible—if someone has facts to check, or writing to complete, we can find someone else to do the extra work. It's about dealing with the challenges on a case by case basis, rather than being Draconian. We're trying to build in flexibility to the system and the new way of working, to make sure that we have choices, to make sure that production qualities remain high.*

Nonetheless, it is our view that the pursuit of digital success is fundamentally transforming the newsroom, and with it the craft of professional journalism, in ways that will have a lasting social and democratic impact.

The organisational and staffing challenges of digital integration are largely being dealt with on an ad hoc basis. Our sense is that there is little in the way of large-scale structural planning or forecasting by news publishers. The aforementioned research by the National Union of Journalists would appear to support that view; ongoing surveys affirm the disenchantment among journalists and correspondents in the way multi-media working is being hurriedly deployed. Even with the considerable performance enhancements afforded by digital technologies, the accuracy and depth of journalism is likely to be impacted as the digital revolution gains momentum, and as publishers seek to retain positions founded in a different economic era. We address each of these points in turn.

7.2. The operational pressures of the digital newsroom are casting a shadow over the factual accuracy of the news

Our discussion of the digital vision and the value chain especially emphasised the generalised pressures that are now facing journalists; namely, the shift in emphasis from newsgathering to processing, and as a result—the prioritization of outputs over inputs (i.e. packaging and distributing the news, as opposed to the gathering and checking of facts). The journalist of the twenty-first century is increasingly required to perform roles that were previously the domain of other specialists; for example, editing, video recording, broadcast presentation.

Combined with the insatiable demands of the 24/7 media, that inevitably means that journalists have less time to travel and meet people in their coverage of stories. The craft of journalism is becoming computer-centric, with search software such as Google mediating the connection between the newsroom and the outside world, and web 2.0 software such as RSS feeds, social networks and blogs funnelling customised news feeds to the desks of editors and journalists alike on an hourly basis. These developments are arguably casting a shadow over the factual accuracy of journalism. The collateral damage of the digital newsroom is the attention of the journalist—and in turn, his or her ability to access the facts and convert that information into a factually accurate story within the time constraints of the 24/7 media.

The danger in this transition is that journalists will make more mistakes, and that those mistakes will proliferate more quickly due to the spontaneity of the web and its interconnectedness with other outlets. In particular, the cross-organizational pooling of resources (which now defines the integrated newsroom) means that content—once deposited in a digital asset management system—is rapidly propagated across channels. In a revealing interview, for example, a prominent MP complained to us that a recent misquote—on a key public policy issue—quickly found its way from print to the web, then a podcast, and eventually a string of other websites.

The permanence and distributed nature of the web also means that it is harder to rectify mistakes once they occur. As we describe below, the Press Complaints Commission is ill-equipped to deal with the expanding territory of the web. In several instances, major news publishers have discovered factoids from the web, and proceeded to use that material in subsequent coverage without fully checking their accuracy—especially when other newsrooms are seen to be doing the same, again reflecting the so-called 'herd mentality' of the news media.[103] The mistakes range in severity, from accreditations in obituaries (as illustrated by the false attribution of an S Club 7 song to BBC television composer, Ronnie Hazlehurst) to dangerous distortions of scientific research (as described well by Ben Goldacre in *Bad Science*).

The incidence of mistakes will depend upon the publisher, and the measures they have in place to mitigate the pressures and inherent fragilities of multimedia working. The problem is likely to be more severe at publishers where cost pressures have resulted in layoffs and knee-jerk attempts at digital integration. The poster child of this digital dystopia is arguably the *Daily Express*, which is poised to remove most of its sub-editors: the critical and final layer of editorial oversight. Lacking the editorial resources needed to fully screen stories, publishers such as the *Daily Express* are likely to suffer a litany of inaccuracies, and potential claims relating to libel and defamation. The broad push for multi-platform productivity carries real dangers:

> *Productivity is going up across the industry—people are doing more work overall. And then there's work placements and interns filling paid jobs working for free. There is increased exploitation of labour … Even at the BBC, where we have had cases of people working for 8 months without a penny. (Jeremy Dear, General Secretary, NUJ)*

There are real concerns about the long-term impacts of cost savings and integration. As one editor observed:

> *It is very difficult at this stage to determine whether we can really achieve the savings without a deterioration in the quality of what we do … the main impact of the budgetary changes overall is time. There's a wear and tear effect on people … that's the biggest concern; that we lose that depth, that reflective journalism.*

The pressures of multimedia working are also resulting in basic spelling and grammatical errors, even at established and otherwise respected news publishers. Writing on the Conservative Home website, activist Graeme Archer worries that declining standards will have a long-term social impact:

---

[103] http://www.telegraph.co.uk/news/newstopics/debates/2964722/
False-internet-rumours-recent-highlights.html

If our leading broadsheet newspapers cannot bother to check the punctuation of one of [their] main news stories, what hope is there for standards anywhere? And doesn't such sloppiness have an impact on the reader? It generates a subliminal response in me: If you can't be bothered to construct your sentences correctly, I'm not bothered to understand the point you're trying to make.[104]

The pressure to publish—combined with the inexorable pursuit of the clickstream—is arguably completing the social transformation of news, which began with satellite television and the advent of rolling news. That transformation radically accentuates the historically contingent and iterative nature of news, with the result that speed is prized more than accuracy to an extent not seen before. For the majority of publishers, the imperative is to define the media agenda, break stories and capture the attention of the audience over as many platforms as possible.

In practice, the vigour of that imperative varies between publishers; for example, weekly newspapers or daily television broadcasts are operating under relatively less pressure compared to digitally integrated news operations which have to feed 24/7 websites or broadcasts. A broadcast executive made the following remarks:

Accuracy is everything to us. It's much more difficult for a 24/7 rolling service to be precise, compared to us—we have more time to respond. For us, it's honesty with the viewer that is crucial. It's about telling the viewer what we do know, and what we can't be sure about. It's not just about right and wrong, but about all the nuances in between. This applies to all our coverage. We give people here the freedom to take a risk; but they equally know that they can't be fast and loose in their coverage, their credibility will suffer as will ours.

In general, though, the news agenda is now prone to more rapid change and updating than ever before. Concerned by this development, Alastair Campbell (Press Secretary to Tony Blair between 1994 and 2003) remarked to the House of Lords Select Committee on Communications that the underlying imperative for speed can have a serious 'impact on any real

---

[104] http://conservativehome.blogs.com/ccntreright/2008/08/the-sad-decline.html

interest in whether the story is right or wrong'.[105] Tim Toulmin (Director of the Press Complaints Commission), however, views this as a changing 'social contract' between news publishers and audiences:

> *I see more inaccuracies in the media in general now but that's because there are more platforms and outlets for journalism. This combined with the fact that things go out quickly. I don't know what the public would think if you asked them to make a choice between getting all of the news accurately but later, or get it all immediately but the story may have to be revised. I suspect they would say that they would want accurate information and wait for it, but in practice I am not sure that this is right.*

It is unclear whether consumers are as accepting of inaccuracy as this view implies. A senior Home Office minister found the concept of deliberately iterative news an 'utterly appalling' proposition. The PCC's own data indicates that the overall volume of complaints has increased by 70 per cent since 1996; and more specifically, that the proportion of complaints relating to the accuracy of the news media (and the opportunity to reply) has also increased, from approximately 55 per cent in 1996 to 77 per cent in 2007.[106]

Some argue that this increase is due to the increased visibility of the PCC or the ease of submitting a complaint via the website. However, our research indicates that the PCC has done relatively little to seriously expand its public profile: for example, it only runs two open days per year (typically for two to three hours on a weekday afternoon) and spends virtually nothing on advertising. With a budget of only £1.8 million, the PCC is materially constrained in its mission to self-regulate an industry that is rapidly expanding onto the web. As many of our interviewees argued, the PCC is a largely ineffectual instrument for meaningful press regulation, particularly in the digital age.

A senior journalist even suggested that the process of PCC intervention is a 'dialogue of the deaf', because of the relatively limited visibility of corrections and apologies in newspapers. Crucially, the PCC lacks the equivalent powers of Ofcom, in the broadcast sector, due to the fundamentally non-scarce nature of newspaper publishing compared to the allocation of TV and radio spectrum. That has fostered a relatively permissive model of industry self-regulation in which errant behaviour by newspapers (ranging

---

[105] House of Lords Select Committee on Communications, *The Ownership of the News,* vol. 1, *Report* (2008), 30.
[106] http://www.pcc.org.uk/annualreport/2007.html

from inaccurate reporting to more egregious abuses, such as intrusion of privacy) attracts only limited censure—in the form of upheld adjudicated decisions, typically buried in the middle of the paper.

In practice, the proportion of cases that actually reach adjudication is minuscule—despite a 347 per cent increase in the number of resolved cases since 1996. In 2007, for example, the PCC received 4,340 complaints; but of those, only 32 reached adjudication; and of those, only 16 were upheld.[107] A growing number of complaints now proceed directly to court, completely bypassing the oversight of the PCC. Even here, however, the press face relatively minor financial penalties.

The damages (£60,000) awarded against the News of the World in the recent Max Mosley case are illustrative. Although a UK record for a privacy claim, £60,000 is clearly a tiny sum for a publisher such as the *News of the World*, for which sensationalist stories (premised on questionable reporting and suspect facts) continue to make perfect economic sense. Neil Wallis (Executive Editor of *NOTW*) emphasised to us the strategic importance of 'big scoops' as a way for tabloids to cushion the impact of falling circulations. A tent-pole story, broken in print, can still generate the circulation spikes necessary to justify the risks and costs of resource allocation.

In other interviews, however, respondents expressed concern about the growth of the 'no win/no fee' legal culture, which threatens to bombard news publishers with more legal action. In a powerful speech to the Society of Newspaper Editors in November 2008, Sir Paul Dacre (Editor of the *Daily Mail*) warned that the result of the 'no win/no fee' culture

> *is that today, newspapers—even wealthy ones like the Mail—think long and hard before contesting actions, even if they know they are in the right, for fear of the ruinous financial implications. For the provincial and local press, such actions are now almost certainly out of the question. Instead, they stump up some cash, money they can't afford, to settle as quickly as possible, to avoid court actions—which, if they were to lose, could, in some cases, close them. Some justice!*[108]

---

[107] As the PCC website describes: 'The Commission can elect formally to adjudicate on any unresolved complaint. This means that the Commission issues a ruling on the substance of the complaint, which is published on this website. If the Commission finds an outstanding breach of the Code, it will uphold the complaint against the publication. The publication will then have to publish the Commission's ruling in full on its pages, with a headline reference to the PCC and with due prominence. If the Commission finds no outstanding breach of the Code, the complaint will be recorded as not upheld.' Sourced from http://www.pcc.org.uk/cases/index.html

[108] http://www.pressgazette.co.uk/story.asp?storycode=42396

For some publishers, there is an editorial as well as a commercial incentive to maintain the accuracy and quality of the news. And as Kenny Campbell (Editor of the *Metro*) noted, the dangers of direct legal action by individuals and organisations also mean that it is in the interests of newspapers to preserve the model of self-regulation enshrined in the PCC.

The permanence of the web—and the rapid proliferation of inaccurate content beyond the digital home base of a newspaper into the blogosphere and beyond—poses a seemingly insurmountable barrier to effective regulation by the PCC. The *regulatory swamp* of convergence is making the situation much worse. As Stewart Purvis (Content and Standards Partner, Ofcom) noted, a 'land grab' is underway as different bodies seek to extend their reach in the digital environment; for example, the PCC is now opening its membership structure to non-newspaper groups, in an effort to promote a kind of 'digital kitemark' that certifies the legitimacy and trustworthiness of news websites, both professional and amateur.

Whilst Ofcom is currently avoiding the regulation of video-enabled newspaper websites, the reach of the European 'Audio-Visual Media Services' Directive will certainly have a bearing on the content of those websites. The purpose of the AVMS is to extend and update the 'Television without Frontiers' Directive of 1989; and in particular, to take into account the shift from 'one-to-many' broadcasting to the 'one-to-one' broadcasting that now prevails on the web. The new directive also reaffirms the basic pillars of Europe's audio-visual model: namely, cultural diversity, protection of minors, consumer protection, media pluralism, and the fight against racial and religious hatred.[109]

Overall, what all of this indicates is that the issue of media accuracy will become more complex and contested as the market funnels precious little resources into the creation of multimedia content, and as regulatory bodies jostle for position in tackling the implications of the digital revolution. There is a risk, however, that the land grab will create a more complex and restrictive regulatory quagmire, in which the agility and competitiveness of news publishers is stifled—particularly compared to foreign or non-commercial publishers operating within different parameters. It is vital, therefore, that a balance is struck between regulatory bodies in the demarcation of boundaries and the oversight of the digital news media:

> *Once boundaries between PCC and Ofcom are established, the difficulty will be not to issue contradictory rulings, information that might confuse the public. For example, if someone is complaining*

[109] http://ec.europa.eu/information_society/newsroom/cf/itemdetail.cfm?item_id=2343

*about Sky News to Ofcom, and it is the same footage as on Telegraph
TV (which we cover), it will be very unsatisfactory if two different
bodies looking at the same objection come up with two completely
different rulings. (Tim Toulmin, Director of the PCC)*

7.3. The digital value chain favours a compressed, personality-driven approach, which threatens to veil the basic facts and context of news stories

Our next point relates more specifically to the depth and substantive
content of journalism in the digital revolution. As multimedia working
continues to erode the attention of journalists, there will be less time available
for the simple reporting and contextualisation of facts, events and stories.
For most publishers, newsgathering is now simply too expensive, as the
reorganisation and net retrenchment of news bureaux at a regional and
international scale demonstrates.

The social cost of that retrenchment is a loss of diversity; spread more
thinly, and pressured by the requirements of multimedia working, the
twenty-first-century journalist will tend to lack the social and cultural
proximity to individuals and organisations that an earlier generation
enjoyed. It was that proximity that allowed the journalists moments of
insight, luck and serendipity. Distanced from the front line, journalists are
less likely to capture and convey the complexity of news stories as they
unfold—thereby enhancing the competitive strengths of those that can
afford to sustain that activity.

Our research finds that the economics of news are increasingly
weighted in favour of comment and opinion, as opposed to the simple
gathering and reporting of facts. As the transformation of the *Independent*
has demonstrated, it is now cheaper and hence more tempting for newspapers to become a *viewspaper*.

Across the news media, there is a growing preference for allocating
space and resources to the production of comment and opinion. In its
recent conversion to a tabloid format, for example, *The Times* expanded
the space allocated to comment and opinion, further eroding the space
available for the reporting of straightforward news. That shift is also
mirrored at other papers and online, where news publishers are busy building
comment-led websites, anchored around celebrity figures and extended
by the audience. Even amidst wider cutbacks and efficiency-savings, news

publishers continue to pay their star commentators what are widely seen as disproportionate salaries.

That trend has sparked a flurry of discontent at the BBC, and also at several commercial publishers, as journalists in general face higher work-loads and hence a net decline in compensation. A telling example is Boris Johnson, who is now reportedly paid £250,000 by the *Daily Telegraph* for a weekly column, an amount that is 82 per cent higher than his salary as Mayor of London. In a dynamic that is congruent with the 'rat pack' effect, news publishers are collectively huddling under the umbrella of celebritised comment as they seek to sharpen and expand their brands to digital audiences. A potential blowback of that strategy, however, may be the disintermediation of news publishers as commentators use the web to connect directly with audiences in the UK and abroad.

To varying degrees, news brands are therefore being 'hollowed out': the underlying civic function of news publishers—to gather information and inform society—is steadily being replaced by a softer, more lightweight model that is dependent on the personal views of a relatively small coterie of heavy-weight commentators and celebrity journalists. Stories and news events are increasingly draped in a celebrity veil in order to capture the attention of the audience; frequently with the assistance of communications and public relations professionals. That is a dangerous trend, as Alan Rusbridger emphasised to us:

> *It all comes back to social responsibility in my view. What is the purpose of the news media if not to produce verifiable facts on which basis people can have an informed debate? If you jump straight to the opinions without having the facts, then society is in trouble.*

The social and democratic impacts of a comment-led news media are myriad. As John Lloyd and Julia Hobsbawm have detailed, the commentariat exerts a powerful influence over public sentiment and policy.[110] Shielded to an extent from editorial oversight, the most powerful commentators are given the latitude to pursue their own style and voice; some even assume a 'cult status', flanked by sycophants as well as detractors. From one angle, this trend is beneficial and entirely rational. Commentators provide a lens through which consumers can view and understand the news:

[110] J. Lloyd and J. Hobsbawm, *The Power of the Commentariat* (2008). http://reutersinstitute.politics.ox.ac.uk/about/news/news_item/article/power_of_the_commentariat_launched_today.html

Nowadays there is greater pressure for analysis and this can stray into comment. Consumers want it—they expect us not just to give the facts but to let them know what we think about the facts. If you look at the sheer coverage of the US primaries, both in comment and in hard news, it is astonishing—perhaps the most covered US election in history. On that level, the press is certainly doing its job rather well. And to differentiate, the papers each week are looking for new angles, new tactics. Overall, I think comment is much stronger. Certainly, the press is less reverential than it was say 50 years ago; it is much more willing to tackle authority, expose corruption, etc. (Simon Jenkins)

From another angle, there are clear drawbacks to the rise of the commentariat. A key area of debate is accountability: some celebrity journalists and star commentators arguably enjoy the status and influence of political figures, but lack the accountability associated with public office. Reinforced by their past successes, these prominent individuals begin to play an instrumental role in the gathering of news and its analysis.

A series of big scoops about the financial crisis have thrown the BBC's Robert Peston into the limelight, for example, with the result that he now enjoys star status, an enviable clickstream record (with over 650,000 hits per day to his blog) and hence significant influence in the reporting of economic policy and related financial developments. In this fashion, the highest-paid stars are quickly emerging as gatekeepers between the news and the public. Their actions directly shape the way individuals, organisations and events are portrayed to the audience. Public sentiment can quickly shift direction, depending on the tone and content of interviews; as demonstrated, for example, by the precipitous decline in Sarah Palin's ratings after her early interview with CBS's Katie Couric.[111]

We emphasise these points to set some context for our discussion in Chapter 8. In our view, it is essential that we begin to raise serious questions about individual as well as organisational accountability in evaluations of media behaviour. (The news media would arguably benefit from a clearly defined set of core standards and values, if only to differentiate professional journalism amidst the competitive noise of the web.)

---

[111] http://www.cbsnews.com/stories/2008/09/24/eveningnews/main4476173.shtml

Another danger associated with the rise of the commentariat is that basic facts and contextual information about news events become suffocated by a cacophony of attention-seeking comment and opinion. As a result, the collateral damage of the digital revolution is not just the attention of the journalist—it is also the attention of the news consumer.

Coupled to the mushrooming blogosphere, the proliferation of comment and opinion on print and broadcast news websites arguably heralds an era of 'infobesity' in which 'our finite attention spans are overwhelmed by infinite information'.[112] In turn, that threatens to render basic facts and contextual information harder to find, and possibly more opaque. In this sense, claims about the commoditisation of news are somewhat overblown. The capabilities of search engines and web aggregators offset that danger to some extent—though as we suggest below, the crowd-powered dynamics of the web threaten a descent into 'echo chambers', where the news agenda is narrowed not broadened.

The point is that audiences increasingly need to be well versed in the basics of a story in order to penetrate and appreciate the increasingly esoteric currents of comment and opinion. Ironically, that entry requirement has increased the appeal of publications such as *The Economist*, which, as Daniel Franklin (Executive Editor) described,

> *seeks to provide in-depth reporting and analysis of curated stories. We see it as an antidote to the bombardment and confusion of the wider media. We provide readers with a shelter, a place where they can enjoy being informed.*

These developments may well be undermining the civic function of the news media. From the perspective of corporate social responsibility, for example, an effective news media would largely be invisible; assuring the transparent delivery of factually accurate news information to citizens. Conveying the facts in this fashion is becoming increasingly difficult for news publishers, due to the cost pressures surrounding newsgathering, as well as related pressures to process news into smaller, snappier and slicker multimedia packages. This leads to our next point: that, in certain quarters, the news media is not only failing in its civic function, but is also exposing citizens to sensationalist coverage, loaded with misleading and harmful information.

---

[112] Kelly, *Red Kayaks and Hidden Gold* (forthcoming).

7.4. The digital revolution strengthens the rationale of sensationalist reporting, limiting debate and exposing the public to 'harmful' news

Until recently, the news media was largely invisible in broader debates about corporate social responsibility. That has now begun to change, thanks to a string of books, articles and seminars concerned with the practices that underpin newsgathering, as well as the real social impact of the news media on the decisions and perceptions of citizens. In common with other corporate citizens, news publishers have the capacity to enrich as well as pollute their immediate environment.[113]

Recent books, such as *Flat Earth News* by Nick Davies or *Bad Science* by Ben Goldacre, have drawn attention to the 'negative externalities' that the news media can and do inflict upon our society. For example, the persistence of suspect newsgathering techniques has inflicted irreparable damage on the relationship between the political establishment and the media, whilst the sensationalism of reporting has warped key issues, thereby limiting the scope of public debate and misinforming citizens.

In light of these issues, we agree there is an urgent need for a clear and systematic appraisal of the social impact of the news media—in particular, because the digital revolution is strengthening the economic rationale of socially and morally questionable behaviour, at least in certain parts of the industry. Our discussion is organised into two sections: first, we consider the specific impact of media behaviour on the reporting and presentation of political debates; second, we look more broadly at some of the likely societal and civic implications of a distorted, PR-focused news agenda.

The news media as a whole have refined an arsenal of newsgathering techniques that are designed to acquire premium and often private information, in spite—or perhaps because—of wider resource constraints. Consequently, the news media occupy an unusually powerful role in the public life of the UK: as one MP remarked, 'they have a more extensive investigatory power than the police, but do not operate under the same constraints'. In his 2006 speech, the *Guardian*'s Alan Rusbridger reflected on the surveillance capabilities of the media:

> *Only the wilfully blind could be oblivious to the widespread concerns people have about the power of the so-called mainstream media. As an editor, I share those concerns. I was rather alarmed by the power I acquired the day, just over 11 years ago, I walked into the*

[113] See J. Bakan, *The Corporation: The Pathological Pursuit of Profit and Power* (Free Press, 2004).

editor's office for the first time. Editors do have the power to make or break people. They can sit as judge and jury on people in public life. They can—or until recently, they could—determine who is allowed a voice in public debate, and who is denied one. They are astonishingly unfettered (compared, say, with any law enforcement agency) to snoop out information on people's private lives. Several British newspapers voice fears about the implications of the Big Brother state—with the prospect of centralised computer databases for security, welfare and health records. In some cases these same newspapers think nothing of paying for exactly the same information about celebrities' private lives using private investigators as cut-outs.[114]

To be sure, an aggressive and innovative news media has social and democratic value: it helps to expose more information overall, and thus holds powerful individuals and organisations to account. In practice, however, much of that aggression tends to be focused on a handful of 'tent-pole' stories—selected through the collective decisions of the 'rat pack'. Moreover, the associated newsgathering activities often transgress even the most basic norms of acceptable behaviour, leading some to argue that parts of the news media are abusing their market position and failing to perform their civic function. This has particular implications for the quality and breadth of the news coverage given to political debates, as well as the ability of citizens to grasp and appreciate the substantive nature and complexities of those debates.

For many years, as John Lloyd and others have argued, the news media and political establishment have been locked in a strikingly dysfunctional relationship.[115] Our research suggests that the underlying dynamics of that relationship are widening and intensifying in the digital revolution. In a series of interviews with prominent figures in media and politics, we were able to identify three key points.

The first and principal area of democratic relevance is the increasingly celebritised and sensationalised nature of political coverage. The end of full parliamentary gallery news coverage in the 1980s arguably marked the beginning of a slippery slope towards shorter, more personality-led stories. At the same time, the definition of what constituted the political agenda shifted, radically over time, from one dictated by government and parliament to one defined by the interaction between the needs of the news

---

[114] http://www.guardian.co.uk/values/socialaudit/story/0,,1926195,00.html
[115] See J. Lloyd, *What the Media are Doing to our Politics* (Constable, 2004).

media for political content and the arguably more urgent need of politicians for coverage.

The multi-channel demands of the current era have accelerated that shift; as we have noted, journalists are under pressure to make their reports slicker and shorter, both for existing channels and the web. By the late 1990s, according to the Goldsmiths Media Research Programme, the average length of time devoted to a television report on political issues in the UK news was *only 23 seconds.*

Crucially, the restructuring of newsrooms is reducing the number of specialist political correspondents in Westminster; those that do cover the political scene are increasingly under pressure to file pieces for a wider range of topics, to an ever wider range of media platforms. As a result, many journalists do not have the time or expertise to cover the true breadth of current political debates, or engage with the substantive material within those debates. (By the same token, however, politicians only have the time to learn about a handful of the policy issues they vote on.) The pressure, instead, is for journalists to focus on the contours of debate through the lens of personality. As another MP noted, the predominant concern is with 'who is up, who is down; it is surprisingly difficult and frustrating to get coverage of key issues'. In a similar vein, Lord Paul Tyler lamented about the increasingly '*Pop Idol*' tone of political coverage. Compounding this issue is the tendency of news coverage to descend into scaremongering (see also, below). As shown by the reporting of UK crime data in July 2008, the content and meaning of government announcements can be easily distorted in an effort to enhance the audience impact of news coverage.

This leads to the second point—that politicians are becoming more guarded in their interaction with the media, which increasingly demands instant comment and opinion around the issues that do achieve space in the news agenda. Because of a tendency to distort and sensationalise, the news media as a whole are finding it harder to obtain public comments from senior figures. In many cases, a press officer now handles comments to the media, adding a further degree of distance between journalists and politicians, and increasing the chances of misunderstanding. Those who do speak directly to the news media carefully manage their message and profile—sometimes in ways that can obscure the debate or bypass known 'ambush points'. As Peter Riddell (Chair of the Hansard Society) lamented,

*Nowadays MPs are more discriminating in who they talk to and
also more Janus faced. They often say what they don't really think
on TV as they no longer have the option of not responding and
mistakes are punished. There is far more reluctance to float a
tentative idea, which may have value in sparking wider debate,
due to fears of being shot down or stigmatised. There is a real
public policy loss as a result of the 24/7 culture.*

The third and final point is that the economic dynamics of the news media
favour the compression of political stories into a more audience-friendly
package, which by necessity tends to detach questions and issues from the
messiness of political debate and related policy research. The sensationalist
tendencies of the news media do little to help the clarification or resolution
of complex social and economic issues. A compounding issue is the
remarkable lack of continuity in news coverage; as Riddell went on to
explain, 'a topic may get coverage one day, then be sidelined from the
agenda—leaving the audience none the wiser about its development'. In
theory, the web has the capacity to address this issue. Coverage of public
interest and otherwise marginal issues can now be continued and extended
online, with links to related coverage and other publicly valuable data. As
we describe in Chapter 8, however, both the news media and the political
establishment are still some way from achieving that degree of visibility,
interactivity and transparency.

The economics that shape the interface between the news media and
the political establishment also have wider social and democratic implications.
Here, we briefly touch upon two issues: the plurality of the news agenda,
and the negative impacts of distorted and sensationalised reporting.

To an extent, the rise of the 24/7, web-enabled multi-channel media
creates new opportunities for otherwise marginal voices—for example,
smaller charities or NGOs—to penetrate the news agenda. By its very
nature, the web enables the tagging, navigation and cross-referencing of
both stories and their stakeholders. In theory this should facilitate increased
exposure for all concerned. In practice, however, the barriers to entry have
risen: competition for exposure and audience attention has led to the rapid
ascendance of communications and public relations skills, as well as related
web marketing and search engine optimisation skills. In turn, this is creating
an uneven playing field that is only open to individuals and organisations

with the requisite profile, message and resources. The following comments were made by senior managers from leading UK charities:

There is a Darwinistic struggle for media attention ... PR is needed to create heat around an issue in the media, so that they can spark a conversation, shape the debate, as well as bring political attention to their cause and associated policy recommendations.

It is getting increasingly difficult to have a national conversation about a topic ... To get your message across now, you have to engage with multiple channels in what is increasingly a fragmented media landscape; and to do that, you need effective PR skills.

At some news publishers, moreover, the pursuit of digital metrics is accentuating the search for audience-friendly stories with traffic-generating potential, irrespective of their public interest value. By default, that approach tends to exclude significant chunks of the social and political spectrum, and favours instead a growing amount of populist trivia (which is drawn, in growing quantities, from specialist PR firms). In its submission to the House of Lords Select Committee in 2007, for example, the Goldsmiths Media Research Programme (led by Professor James Curran) stated:

There has been a decline in expensive forms of news coverage and ... a greater 'tabloidisation' of news ... Celebrity and entertainment stories made up 17% of news in 1997, up from 6% in 1952 ... [There has been a] removal or repackaging of 'serious news' and an increase in light features. Soundbite summaries are common.[116]

The stories that do penetrate the news agenda, however, are frequently imbued with a large amount of blame, negativity or sensationalism, which obscures the real issues and misinforms citizens. There is an urgent need, in our view, for a wider and more serious debate about the potential dangers of distorted news coverage. Much of the news media is prone to this behaviour, in large part to maximise the impact of their coverage. The rise of PR is also a factor, as we have already suggested. To differentiate themselves from the positive overtones of PR, journalists are increasingly veering into a cul de sac of scaremongering and fear-driven speculation about the future. A strong critic of this issue, Lord Clive Soley commented:

the continual resort to scaremongering creates an exaggerated fear factor in one part of society; the other half switch off and feel they are powerless. There is a need to give space to other news and views as a counterpoint.

What this underscores is the very real impact of the news media on the decisions, perceptions and fears of citizens. There is scope for considerable confusion and misunderstanding, notably in poorer areas with lower levels of media literacy, or in older demographics.

Nowhere is this clearer than in the area of health reporting. In his recent book, *Bad Science*, the GP and journalist Ben Goldacre eloquently outlines the dangers to public health arising from sensationalised, PR-driven and unsubstantiated reporting.[117] Examples range from the coverage of Kylie Minogue's breast cancer (which led, virtually overnight, to a 40 per cent increase in mammogram bookings) to the staged coverage of drug trials (such as Herceptin) or the media's obsession with peculiar illnesses and superficial magic cures (which necessarily eclipse serious stories and sensible lifestyle advice). As he shows, health risks are frequently fuelled and peddled by parts of the media without reference to any legitimate data or medical testimony. The underlying message is that bad information about health-related issues can kill people:

People make health decisions based on what they read in the newspapers ... there can be no doubt that the appalling state of health reporting is now a serious public health issue ... The media created the MMR hoax, and they maintained it diligently for 10 years. Their failure to recognise that fact demonstrates that they have learned nothing, and until they do, journalists and editors will continue to perpetrate the very same crimes, repeatedly, with increasingly grave consequences.[118]

To be sure, the combination of effective PR with responsible media coverage can also deliver social value. For example, the orchestration of disease awareness campaigns can radically broaden understanding of an issue and potentially save lives in the process. In 2008 alone, an estimated 460,000 lives have been saved in the UK thanks to a variety of government

---

[117] B. Goldacre, *Bad Science* (Fourth Estate, 2008).
[118] http://www.guardian.co.uk/society/2008/aug/30/mmr.health.media, extracted from Goldacre, *Bad Science*.

initiatives designed to help people quit smoking. That kind of success is explicitly dependent on the effective dissemination of information via the media, and with the assistance of PR experts.

In a balanced form, where there is transparent labelling of sources, the media can therefore help to avoid and mitigate the public harm associated with excessively sensationalised reporting. Like other industries, the news media needs to be far more cognizant of its responsibility as a purveyor of information that directly shapes and impacts the lives of citizens.

In fact, the digital revolution also creates new opportunities for the news media to invigorate and strengthen the engagement between citizens and democratic processes. It is to this issue that we turn in Chapter 8. The long-term challenge is imagining and designing a more networked, transparent conception of the news media, which is not only built upon the contributions of professional journalists but also upon the insights, knowledge and skills of citizens, charities, companies, campaigners, government agencies, NGOs, and other stakeholders.

8. Digital possibilities

In our view, there is an urgent need for a dispassionate and sustained debate about the civic function of the news media in modern democracies, especially as publishers respond to the commercial challenges of the digital revolution.

In the quest for digital success, publishers are following a path towards efficiency, cost-control and integration that is likely to be riddled with a series of democratic potholes. In the previous chapter, we outlined the form and potential significance of those potholes in the context of the UK. Our analysis is by no means definitive or comprehensive; nor is it meant to imply the existence of an earlier golden age. Nonetheless, we do believe that the scope of the digital revolution, and the emerging directions of change among publishers, point towards fundamental changes in both the economics and craft of professional journalism. Those changes have the capacity to erode the civic function of the UK news media in ways that demand attention from a public policy standpoint.

In this chapter, we outline possible steps that might be taken to minimise or at least offset the *democratic deficit* of a digitally integrated news media. We present these steps as potential navigational waypoints on the road ahead—not as definitive end points or perfect solutions—which academics, journalists, executives, regulators and citizens may wish to consider. It is our hope that the findings in this report, and the recommendations outlined below, will serve as a foundation for follow-on seminars, workshops and other comparative studies. The principal goal of this report is to stimulate further debate and research on the commercial and civic side of the equation. Our discussion focuses on both sides of this equation.

First, we consider (via section 8.1) the steps that might be taken to ensure the continued provision of what we generically term 'quality' news in the UK—that is, *balanced, independent, reliable reporting of matters of public interest.* Here, we draw attention to the different funding pools necessary for news publishers to fulfil the rudimentary elements of their civic function. As we show, it may be possible for government to encourage the continued investment into newsgathering by reviewing the structure and conditions of UK taxation and charitable law. For example, targeted tax breaks could be used to incentivise the investment of private capital— by individuals and organisations—into the craft of professional journalism, both for sustained reporting and longer term investigative work.

Second, we then consider (via sections 8.2 and 8.3) the steps that might be taken to nurture the creation and renewal of an informed and participatory digital citizenry, with suggestions targeting news publishers, government and also citizens themselves. The digital age heralds a far more transparent and collaborative public sphere: never before in history have citizens had such easy, instant access to such enormous quantities of original source material, emanating from government, NGOs and other entities. The net impact of these changes may, in fact, be a *democratic windfall* rather than a democratic deficit—but when or how that might be realised is open to debate.

The next generation news media have the capacity to recast themselves as a professional hub within a broader, more distributed and transparent network of quasi-news suppliers, stretching from the sophistication of the public relations industrial complex to the raw energy of citizen journalism. As we have suggested, the future is especially bright for what we've called digital anchors, given their ability to aggregate a complementary federation of content, consumers and advertising around a brand voice. In this form, moreover, the news media have the capacity to meet commercial goals whilst also performing a valuable civic function.

8.1. To safeguard the provision of public interest news, the government should review the conditions and structure of UK taxation and charitable law

The commercial pressures of the digital revolution raise pressing questions about the long-term civic function of the news media—in particular, its ability to hold powerful individuals, institutions and organisations to account, and to perform the sustained monitoring of society from a local to national scale.

To be sure, the scope and practical meaning of that civic function are interpreted in widely different ways by publishers; for example, the *News of the World* would articulate its role in society differently from the *Guardian*. Notwithstanding the questionable tactics sometimes employed by some publishers, the net benefit of an enquiring news media is clear: it exposes information, holds those in power to account, contributes to debate and enables citizens to make informed decisions. The civic virtues of a free and unconstrained news media overwhelmingly militate against any form of government censorship or restriction of expression.

But the civic function of the news media simply cannot be separated from underlying economic realities. Across the industry, the value of established media channels is crumbling faster than publishers can build viable digital alternatives. As we have shown, news publishers are pursuing a digital vision that weakens, to varying degrees, the efficacy of that civic function. As more publishers morph into digital windsocks, the short-term imperatives of commercial survival will take precedence over the longer term questions of societal responsibility. In the years ahead, there will be relatively fewer commercial publishers able to contemplate—let alone fully realise—that civic function.

The challenges of the digital revolution will only become more acute in the coming recession. As some commentators have predicted, that risks a dramatic contraction of the news media, over the next two to five years, perhaps comparable in severity to the famous shakeout of British newspapers during the interwar years.[119]

There is a generalised pressure, affecting digital windsocks and anchors alike, which favours a strategic focus on the processing rather than the generation of original content. As resources dwindle, for example, publishers are opting for a greater proportion of *confirmatory* as opposed to *initiatory* journalism in their overall news mix. This is because the net revenue per journalist appears to be in decline; and as a result, publishers cannot afford to commit resources to the sustained monitoring and reporting of society, at home and abroad. To attract the interest of global audiences, however, news publishers need a growing amount of content; as such, they are populating their websites with content from news wires, public relations gatekeepers, star commentators and the emerging army of citizen journalists. The overall point, therefore, is that the continued, systematic gathering and provision of reliable news—a vital prerequisite to the creation and renewal of an informed citizenry—appears to be under threat. Key areas such as coverage of political debate, foreign news or investigative reports

[119] http://www.guardian.co.uk/media/2008/oct/20/pressandpublishing-emilybell

are under strain due to the scarcity of resources. There are relatively few havens, outside the shelter of the BBC, the specialised newspapers and the Scott Trust, where the costs and complexities of a multi-channel news operation can be managed in a fashion that does not impair the civic function of the news.

Even in those havens, the editorial staff are facing similar pressures, not least because media executives are lured by the logic of integration and the visibility of clickstream metrics. The distinctive characteristics of the digital marketplace mean that it is unlikely to ever provide a sufficiently robust economic foundation; instead, varieties of cross-subsidy will be required to fill the gap. The realities of the digital revolution mean that only diversified media groups can afford to commit significant resources to (and effectively cross-subsidise) both the generation and processing of news.

What is needed, in our view, is a clear, dispassionate and measured government review of the potential funding pools that might be able to subsidise the continued provision of quality news in the UK—to reiterate, news that offers citizens a balanced, independent and reliable account of events of public interest. Echoing Lord Stephen Carter's earlier comments, this review should focus on finding ways in which we can supplement the public value of the BBC with a diverse and digitally viable ecology of commercial news publishing. Significantly, we believe that this review should also take into account two further points.

The first is that a pluralistic ecology of news publishing would have beneficial *spill over* effects for independent media production across the UK. By helping to secure the creative future of commercial news publishers, in addition to the BBC, the government would also be securing a vital source of revenue for independent producers of news (including daily reports, documentaries and investigative pieces), who are supported to a considerable degree by contracts with the BBC and other publishers. Under the terms of their current licence, for example, the main terrestrial television channels are required to source a specific quota of their total output from independent producers and from outside London.[120] With a more stable economic footing, publishers would be able to divert extra resources to the independent community; indeed, such a quota system could be explicitly applied to the provision of news, to widen the sectoral and geographic range of any spill over effect.[121]

---

[120] http://www.ofcom.org.uk/consult/condocs/psb2_1/
[121] As we mentioned earlier, for example, the efficiencies derived from the processing of news have recently enabled Channel 4 news to increase the resources allocated to its 'Independents Fund'.

The second and related point is that any government review should recognise the societal benefits of both long-term (investigative-based) forms of reporting and short-term (monitoring-based) forms of reporting. As Charlie Beckett recently wrote,

> *Good reliable, independent, routine reporting can have a bigger impact in the medium and long-term than a one-off scoop revelation. Journalism as a whole has a watchdog role.*[122]

With this as a backdrop, we believe it is worthwhile considering the potential role that government might play in encouraging continued investment into both areas of newsgathering. In particular, our research indicates that the UK government could potentially pull various legislative *levers* that might make it more appealing for individuals and organisations to spend their time and money on the professional gathering and reporting of news. In our view, there is scope for a review of UK tax law and charitable law. To be sure, the changes we propose would have far-reaching impacts and would therefore require more detailed assessment, not only to optimise their viability but also to prevent any undesirable side effects. These changes might supplement alternative funding arrangements, including those currently being explored—for example, Ofcom's proposition (in its latest public service review) that consortia of newspapers, broadcasters and others might bid for the competitive funding of national, regional and local news.[123]

The first proposed area of change is an extension and strengthening of tax concessions in the UK news media. At present, for example, UK newspapers enjoy a zero rating for value-added tax (VAT), alongside other goods and services that the government deems eligible (including books, food, children's clothes and disabled equipment) due to their benefit to society. The government might therefore consider extending that kind of status to the wider converged news media—in recognition of the cyclical and structural challenges facing news publishers, and of the civic benefits of a diverse and economically robust ecology of commercial news websites alongside the BBC. In practice, this might entail the extension of zero-related VAT status to the sale of advertising space on news websites, the reduction of tax on digital income, both for newspapers and broadcasters, or more general tax breaks relating to the costs of staffing and maintaining an integrated newsgathering operation.

[122] http://www.charliebeckett.org/?p=666
[123] Ofcom, *Second Public Service Broadcasting Review: Preparing for the Digital Future* (2008), 77: http://www.ofcom.org.uk/consult/condocs/psb2_phase2/

The purpose would be to minimise the current disparity between the costs and revenue-generating potential of news websites. To have civic value, however, such tax changes might need to relate specifically to those parts of the website that provide coverage of core categories of public interest news (e.g. political, economic, social justice, environment). In other words, publishers might be guaranteed some form of tax break on income derived from public interest web content.

How such a system would be designed and implemented is necessarily a question for subsequent debate and research. A potential pitfall would be reaching mutually acceptable standards about what constitutes public interest news—and hence, what qualifies for any related tax exemption or special treatment. In addition, the regular monitoring (of content) required of such a system might be argued to infringe on the basic freedoms of the news media. It might be more appropriate, therefore, to sever any connection between the provision (or amount) of government support and the specific content (or perceived civic value) of the news output—or at the very least, contemplate a model premised upon self-regulation. As we summarise below, it is not government's place to award prizes for good behaviour in the news media, no matter how desirable that behaviour might be from a civic standpoint.

The second proposed change is a review of the legislative framework around charitable giving. Compared to other developed countries, for example, the UK lacks the financial and political ingredients necessary for large-scale philanthropic support of professional journalism.

At present, a major stumbling block is the most recent Charities Act of 2006, which adopts a stringent interpretation of *public benefit* that excludes any reference to newsgathering.[124] There are UK journalism-related charities, to be sure—the Thomson Reuters Foundation, which backs the host of this report, the Reuters Institute, being a notable and important example. But the practical reality is that the Charities Commission tends to view the pursuit of journalism—namely, the professional gathering and reporting of news—as an inherently politicised activity and hence an area less suited for charitable giving. Martin Moore described to us the frustrating 'uphill battle' that the Media Standards Trust faced in achieving charitable status. Similarly, Gavin MacFadyean lamented the fact that he had to hire a specialist legal team (at a crippling cost) to justify the charitable dimensions of his organization, the Centre for Investigative Journalism.

---

[124] http://www.charity-commission.gov.uk/publicbenefit/default.asp

As a result, the UK today has only a handful of news media-related charities engaged in the substantive work of professional newsgathering. The legal context therefore needs review. That might entail three areas of change. First, loosening the definition of public benefit to include journalism, and hence simplifying the certification of news media-related charities. Second, designing tax breaks to encourage the donation of money to such activity, by organisations and wealthy individuals. Third, extending the VAT-exempt status of charitable fundraising to news media-related charities.

As the commercial pressures of the digital revolution intensify, the democratic deficit created by an impoverished news media could be filled—to some small extent—by an extension and deepening of charitable activity, especially in the area of investigative or community reporting. Practically, however, there are significant cultural and institutional barriers in the UK, which lags significantly behind other countries in the overall level of philanthropy—notably, the tax benefits that accrue from charitable giving, or the presence of philanthropic institutions and foundations.

In the United States, for example, the situation is radically different. There, a variety of richly endowed charitable organisations—such as the Alicia Patterson, Annenberg and Knight Foundations, the Pew Charitable Trusts, Nieman Fellowship programme at Harvard, or the Poynter Institute—provide support and funding for journalism and the news media in all their guises, through training, awards, research, grants, fellowships and bursaries. There are no comparable examples in the UK. We do not pretend to imagine that changes in UK charity law will trigger a surge of philanthropy, thereby saving journalism overnight. Nonetheless, a simplification of the rules surrounding charitable giving may provide a valuable impetus to news media-related philanthropy, and thereby open up alternative funding pool for news and potentially enable a more pluralistic ecology of news media to develop.

Depending on the tax breaks, that might encourage media organisations to support a range of charitable activities, either internally or externally through partnerships—with a prime example being the support given to Global Voices in the US by the Thomson Reuters Corporation. In addition to the substantive work of newsgathering, such activities might also include training, investigative fellowships or awards. A specific outcome of any legislative review might be the creation of a sponsored charitable prize fund designed to foster technological innovations around the craft of journalism in the digital age. In the US, for example, the Knight Foundation supports an annual 'News Challenge' through which prizes are awarded to entrepreneurs creating novel business models. A recent winner was David Cohn's Spot.us, which was awarded $340,000 over two years to pilot a distributed 'crowd-powered' approach to the funding of news.

In practical terms, the evaluation and certification of potential news-related charities would require some form of regulatory oversight. The Charities Commission, or the Inland Revenue, might perform such a function, ideally in an arms-length or apolitical fashion. A vital consideration to take into account is the question of conditionality—that is, there is a potential danger is that the conferment of charitable status would become conditional upon various restrictions or expectations, potentially shaped by government. In effect, the charitable funding of news would be dependent upon both government support and indirect public funding (through the opportunity cost of reduced tax revenues).

As Lord Stephen Carter recently commented, 'with public funding comes a new set of obligations'.[125] The danger of such obligations is that they might impair or warp the work and direction of journalists and publishers, whether in a stand-alone charity or a commercial setting. Our view is that the provision of any government support—via a review of taxation or charitable law—should come without strings attached. To preserve the freedom and investigative inquiry of the news media, a self-regulatory approach is favoured.

8.2. The visibility and civic value of news on the web could benefit from a voluntary 'digital kitemark', oriented around accountability and transparency

The digital generation is literally awash with information. In the next five years alone, we will allegedly produce more information—in a form that can be stored and indexed via the web—than in the entire preceding history of human civilisation. That digital tsunami is captured by the growth rates of popular websites: You Tube's repository is growing by 18,720 hours per day, Flickr by 4 million photos per day, Wikipedia by 1,400 articles per day, and the web as a whole by a remarkable 1 billion pages per day.[126] By any measure, the digital age embodies an unprecedented abundance of choice, in stark contrast to the artificial scarcity of the mass media age. The rise of a new generation of digital natives should, therefore, herald a new

---

[125] http://www.bbc.co.uk/radio4/factual/mediashow/mediashow_20081105.shtml
[126] http://www.cisco.com/web/about/ac123/ac147/archived_issues/ipj_11-2/112_evolution.html

and more engaged and educated citizenry, which is able to make informed decisions on the basis of ample evidence, news and opinion. However, two key issues are likely to puncture that utopian vision.

The first is the persistence (and likely endurance) of a *digital divide*. The transition from mass media to new media will be geographically and socially uneven, making issues of access and digital equity vital from a policy standpoint (as Lord Stephen Carter's forthcoming *Digital Britain* report identifies). Nonetheless, as computing and communications become cheaper, it is plausible to assume that, at a certain point in the future, the majority of citizens will use digital platforms in some form to access the news.

The second is the *crowd-powered* dynamic of the web, which can blinker not broaden the world-view of citizens. This point is especially pertinent to our analysis. As more consumers turn to digital platforms for their news and information, there are understandable concerns about where their attention is spent, whether that even includes news, and how the digital news agenda is shaped. The 'centripetal' structure of the web means that attention is increasingly focused around a few sites—oriented, mainly, around social networking, shopping and fantasy—and that news is relatively marginalised.

As we have mentioned, there is evidence of a digital dystopia emerging around news on the web. In the search for clicks, news publishers are under pressure to conform to the windsock model, which favours the processing of 'softer' audience-friendly content over the gathering of 'harder' public interest content. The digital revolution favours the compression of news stories into personality-oriented packages, which are not necessarily conducive to the adequate treatment of complex issues and debates. In a sea of information, it is only logical that consumers turn to trusted brands, including the familiar face of star commentators and columnists, for an analysis of the news.

That is compounded by the atomised and scattered nature of online news consumption, which increasingly means that more consume news à la carte, via search results and RSS feeds. The unique customisation capabilities of the on-demand web threaten a descent into customised echo chambers (or what Charles Leadbeater terms 'cultural boltholes'[127]) in which citizens are exposed to only a fraction of the actual news—a phenomenon that Nicholas Negroponte presciently termed the 'Daily Me' in his 1995 book, *Being Digital*.[128]

---

[127] C. Leadbeater, *We Think: The Power of Mass Creativity* (Profile Books, 2008).
[128] N. Negroponte, *Being Digital* (Vintage, 1995)

Research supports this general trend. In a survey of 1,400 political blogs, for example, Cass Sunstein discovered that 91 per cent linked to like-minded sites.[129] A similar dynamic is even underway in academic and scientific circles. In a recent paper for *Science*, James Evans found that 'as more journals and articles came online, the actual number of them cited in research decreased, and those that were cited tended to be of more recent vintage'.[130] What this suggests, as technology writer Nicholas Carr has observed, is that the direction and extent of web-based inquiry tends to be more superficial:

> *When the efficiency ethic moves from the realm of goods production to the realm of intellectual exploration, as it is doing with the Net, we shouldn't be surprised to find a narrowing rather than a broadening of the field of study. Search engines, after all, are popularity engines that concentrate attention rather than expanding it, and, as Evans notes, efficiency amplifies our native laziness.*[131]

Whether search engines such as Google are changing our neurology and 'making us stupid', as Carr argued in a separate article, is a fascinating topic for further debate and scientific research.[132] A recent study at UCLA's Memory and Aging Research Centre, for example, indicated that

> *for computer-savvy middle aged and older adults, searching the internet triggers key centres in the brain that control decision-making and complex reasoning. The findings demonstrate that Web search activity may help stimulate and possibly improve brain function.*[133]

All that we can flag at this point are the inherent dangers of a platform where 'popularity engines' are emerging as the principal gatekeepers between news and the citizen. The algorithmic myopia of that platform makes it vulnerable to democratic failure in at least two general ways.

The first is that the trails of the clickstream of news consumption are unlikely to produce an accurate and balanced news agenda. In fact, the reverse is often true. In September 2008, for example, the dangers of an automated approach to news were brought to the fore when an outdated

---

[129] http://www.salon.com/news/feature/2007/11/07/sunstein/
[130] http://www.britannica.com/blogs/2008/08/research-web-more-consensus-less-diversity-at-least-sofar/
[131] http://www.roughtype.com/archives/2008/08/easy_does_it.php
[132] http://www.theatlantic.com/doc/200807/google
[133] http://newsroom.ucla.edu/portal/ucla/ucla-study-finds-that-searching-64348.aspx

article (about United Airlines filing for bankruptcy in 2002) was accidentally given prominence by Google News—in turn alarming investors and sparking a $1 billion run on UA's stock. The Securities and Exchange Commission is now conducting a preliminary investigation into the fiasco, which saw UA's stock slump from $12 to $3 per share.[134]

Another reason for concern is that the open structure of the web means it is vulnerable to appropriation and manipulation by special interests. In a context where clicks represent the currency of success, massaging the digital profile of content (through search engine optimisation) can pay off handsomely. Elsewhere, entrepreneurial software writers have devised ways of creating a black market in digital votes—a notable illustration being Subvert and Profit, a website that sells ratings on social media properties such as Digg, iLike, Newsvine, StumbleUpon and You Tube.[135]

From a democratic angle, therefore, the web exhibits a series of structural dangers—not only as a platform for news, but also and more critically, as a channel that shapes the world-view of citizens. There is clear scope for interventions that are designed not only to minimise these dangers but also to maximise the democratic potential that the web has to offer citizens—as related initiatives such as Sir Tim Berners-Lee's Web Science Research initiative have also emphasised.[136] In practice, the echo chamber of digital consumption is never completely impermeable to outside opinion, as the unpredictability and serendipity of web communication attests. BBC columnist Bill Thompson notes:

> The [internet] filters I make for myself are imperfect in just the right way, because they let my friends' interests and activities percolate through and ensure that I'm kept aware of things that are important but which I am not especially interested in. In that sense they replicate the serendipity that comes from reading news-papers, but in a more nuanced way.[137]

Arguably its greatest single benefit, the web reduces the barriers to communication to an unprecedented extent—enabling otherwise marginal voices to find their audience. Outside the UK, the effects of digital liberation are particularly marked in authoritarian states, where the censors of mass media are struggling to plug the holes in the rapidly expanding architecture of the internet (due mainly to the availability of

---

[134] http://technology.timesonline.co.uk/tol/news/tech_and_web/article4742147.ece
[135] http://subvertandprofit.com/
[136] http://webscience.org/
[137] http://news.bbc.co.uk/1/hi/technology/7617207.stm

proxy servers and encrypted file-sharing networks, such as Freenet). In democratic societies, the web has provided a stimulus to debate and participation, and may provide, as Yochai Benkler suggests in *The Wealth of Networks*, the framework for a more egalitarian and networked public sphere.[138] Never before have citizens been able to connect with elected representatives as easily or as quickly.

Through its various initiatives, for example, MySociety is emerging as a sort of twenty-first-century news organisation; by providing open tools and platforms, it enables citizens to stay abreast of the issues in their neighbourhood and radically simplifies the process of democratic participation. In its latest project, GroupsNearYou.com, MySociety is analysing the geographic foci of Yahoo! Groups, enabling users to search for news and discussions by postcode. The overall implication is that the web can refigure the relationship between citizens, government and the media in ways that may yield a substantial democratic windfall.

We can group our own recommendations into two categories. The first (addressed in this section) relates specifically to the work of journalists and news publishers. The provision (and indeed, visibility) of 'quality news' in the UK might benefit from a voluntary and clearly defined set of media standards, oriented around principles of accountability and transparency.

The collective positioning of publishers around these standards might serve as the anchor for a digital kitemark—perhaps represented visually and electronically, as embedded metadata—which would be designed to identify and differentiate professional journalism amidst the noise of the web. With the support of a search engine such as Google, such a kitemark might be used to flag, filter and foreground public interest news. In fact, the *algorithmic myopia* of current internet search technologies—that is, their focus on the hyperlink, rather than the context in which that link is used— would potentially make the kitemark a valuable addition to the inner workings of Google, Yahoo and others. As Martin Moore (Director of the Media Standards Trust) has argued, there is a

> *clear and logical need for the intelligent labelling of digital news— in much the same way that the ingredients and nutritional information of food are communicated to consumers . . .*

In its Transparency Initiative, for example, the Media Standards Trust is hoping to pioneer the deployment of open source software tags, embedded

---

[138] Y. Benkler, *The Wealth of Networks: How Social Production Transforms Markets and Freedom* (Yale University Press, 2006).

in news media content on the web. The purpose of this metadata would be to communicate basic contextual information to consumers—namely, who produced the content, whether it was commissioned or created on behalf of another individual or organisation, whether it was edited and by whom, when it was published, and where it was created. In this fashion, the Media Standards Trust hopes to create a radically new system of transparency that is shaped and implemented from the bottom–up, rather than from the top–down.

In time, a digital kitemark built around transparency might also incorporate a more general set of principles and values—possibly relating to editorial and journalistic codes of conduct. In fact, an open source approach may offer a more robust and feasible route to the articulation of industry codes. There is a pressing need, especially, for more content specific codes of conduct. The prevailing PCC code, for example, offers a monolithic and service-based umbrella code that fails to take into account the wide array of content that newspapers and others are now creating for their digital platforms. It is reasonable to assume that publishers and journalists may prefer to link to different codes of conduct for different forms of coverage—for example, political reporting versus travel and leisure writing. The web, by comparison, fosters a more dynamic and organic approach to the articulation of industry codes.

The benefits of transparency and accountability are myriad. For publishers, adherence to a transparent process of labelling might help to differentiate their news from other websites. Paired with a kitemark, an indicator of digital transparency could convey to the audience that the content offered on a website had been subjected to a rigorous series of checks, and further, had been created by a professional journalist employed to write in a specific field of coverage—as opposed to a blogger, writing for free and outside any formal editorial process or code of conduct.

As we suggested earlier, this strategy might also serve to sharpen the general 'brand' of professional journalism. In theory, publishers who choose to associate themselves with the kitemark may also decide to collectively form something akin to a 'digital free trade area', in which they forge mutual links between related content. Anne Spackman of Times Online views that form of collective partnership as a logical approach to the web. Professor Robert Picard concurs, suggesting that in future publishers will need to specialise to some degree by anchoring their brand in a specific—but potentially global—niche of the market. Jeff Jarvis argues that publishers should 'cover what they do best and link to the rest'.[139]

[139] http://www.buzzmachine.com/2007/02/22/new-rule-cover-what-you-do-best-link-to-the-rest/

For citizens, the benefits of transparency are also wide-ranging. In our view, the transparent labelling of news content would convert the news media into a more visual and navigable form—on which citizens would be able to make more informed decisions about their social, economic and political lives. The addition of descriptive metadata would also improve the accuracy and relevance of search engines such as Google. For example, had the earlier story about United Airlines been tagged with simple metadata about its publication date, the algorithms of Google News would have been able to discern that it was outdated—thereby avoiding the subsequent fiasco. Metadata would also lay the foundations for more effective semantic enrichment of stories, as well as the verification and development of story threads by readers themselves. Which leads us to the next group of recommendations.

8.3. To nurture an informed and participatory digital citizenry, government and civic education should be redesigned to harness the potential of the web

Civic empowerment will depend to a significant degree upon the availability and transparency of publicly funded data. In an open, navigable format, public data has the potential to act as a catalyst around which distributed modes of reporting can take hold, which enrol the skills of both professional and citizen journalists. The UK government can contribute to the development of better informed citizens, and a more networked Fourth Estate, in two critical ways.

The first is simply by releasing more data in more easily accessible electronic formats about the structure, operation and performance of publicly funded bodies. In the UK, there are currently over 100,000 public bodies, each generating terabytes of data each year that could be accessed and used over the internet. Much of that data still remains invisible to the population, despite the implementation of the Freedom of Information Act.

MP Tom Watson argues that there is a pressing need for government to build and extend public data from the bottom–up, in an organic and collaborative fashion.[140] Indeed, our research finds that there is a compelling case for opening the doors of government to far greater scrutiny, given the potential economic and social welfare benefits of fully searchable public data.[141]

---

[140] http://news.bbc.co.uk/1/hi/technology/7720604.stm
[141] E. Mayo and T. Steinberg, *The Power of Information: An Independent Review* (2008): http://www.opsi.gov.uk/advice/poi/index

From an economic angle, public data already provide a platform for a remarkably diverse array of activities. For example, the Ordnance Survey (OS) estimates that its mapping data underpins over £100 billion of economic activity, due to the integral role of route planning and postcode locations to a range of logistical and delivery oriented businesses.[142] In other areas, there is scope for valuable public data to be made available on a commercial and non-commercial basis. Recent studies have indicated that, if public data were made more accessible using the internet, the UK government could double its commercial licensing revenues from £590 million to over £1 billion annually.

It should be noted, however, MySociety and Free our Data argue that the cost and restrictions of OS licences are excessive—especially in light of the fact that its underlying information base was originally compiled with taxpayers' money.[143] OS continues to restrict a variety of publicly valuable mapping activities, including those devised by local authorities and individual citizens.[144] Wider adoption of non-commercial licenses and open APIs (application programming interfaces) would provide a foundation on which other enterprises and citizen-led innovation could flourish. The Ordnance Survey's Open Space initiative is a step in that direction, as is the BBC's 'Back Stage' project, which enables internet users to develop new applications and services around BBC content.

From a social welfare angle, the benefits are also clear. Across the internet, users are busy creating a series of *digital commons* that address the interests and needs of particular social groups, some of which may be underserved by conventional government initiatives.[145] In some cases, tiny groups of users have created successful websites that are now regularly used by tens of thousands of citizens—for example, Net Mums, run from a home in North London for mothers.[146] Meanwhile, 'Show us a Better Way', a recent web-based competition spearheaded by MP Tom Watson, highlighted the ingenuity and enthusiasm of users in exploring public data.[147]

As internet use expands, it is becoming increasingly apparent that, in certain situations, citizens are capable of producing online information resources that are equal or superior (in terms of breadth, quality and relevance) to government equivalents. There are grounds for government to support such citizen-led initiatives—notably, by enhancing access to the

---

[142] http://www.ordnancesurvey.co.uk/oswebsite/media/features/introos/
[143] http://www.freeourdata.org.uk/index.php
[144] http://www.guardian.co.uk/technology/2008/nov/20/ordnance-survey-google-maps
[145] See D. Bollier, *Viral Spiral: How the Commoners Built a Digital Republic of their Own* (New Press, 2009).
[146] http://www.netmums.com
[147] http://www.showusabetterway.com

underlying public data that would likely enrich such initiatives. It is also clear that, collectively, networks of internet users are able to find new, previously untried ways of utilising and interpreting public data, improving its net value to society. The ongoing juxtaposition of different data points on online maps (known as 'mash ups') is a powerful illustration.

In relation to the news media specifically, the provision of public data would help to build new connections between the coverage of democratic processes and the actual practice of those processes. In the citizen's eye, that would almost certainly enhance the breadth, relevance, continuity and interactivity of news coverage, both in the mainstream media and in the interstices of new media. Indeed, quasi-newsgathering organisations such as MySociety effectively bypass the existing news media.

The democratic value of recent online initiatives, for example, derives from their ability to let users easily browse through data by criteria such as topic, geographical region, or individual MP; in turn, making elements of the political landscape far more accessible than was hitherto possible. The next generation of search tools (e.g. semantics, sentiment) will bring about even more effective and targeted navigation of data.

But internet search is still largely text-dominated. There are vast amounts of data, encoded in video, audio or photographic form, which are still resistant to automated navigation. For the time being, such data relies on human-led forms of classification; again underscoring the collaborative power of the internet and the scope for citizen-led initiatives. For example, TheyWorkForYou.com recently launched an innovative database of parliamentary videos: the software enables users to watch brief video clips of debates and questions, so that the underlying *Hansard* transcript can be matched with the appropriate chunk of video data. In just 10 days, a cohort of dedicated internet users classified over 40 per cent of the initial video archive.[148] Such a model could easily be extended to other areas of data; at least until software enabling the artificial simulation and classification of video and audio feeds reaches commercial viability.

The second way the government can accelerate the development of a more transparent and distributed form of news media is by opening itself to more inquiry and engagement through the power of digital technology. It is here that the opportunities and challenges are perhaps the greatest.

On the one hand, governments now have the capacity to use technology to recast democracy in a new light and a new mould, as Barack Obama has sought to illustrate in the US. By reconfiguring internal systems and

---

[148] http://news.bbc.co.uk/1/hi/technology/7433142.stm

rendering transparent the labyrinthine structure of government decision-making, both Houses of Parliament could achieve a new level of interactivity with UK citizens. In particular, digital media could be utilised to democratise knowledge and understanding of the processes through which policy is formed and enacted—and thereby convey to citizens the specific points at which they can make a real difference.

A change of this magnitude would require a complete overhaul of government systems, so that they were designed and built anew from the perspective of the citizen rather than the bureaucracy. As our interviews with Members of Parliament and Peers confirmed, the structure and culture of government is inherently resistant to such transparency for institutional and generational reasons. The changes we describe would puncture the veil of mystery that surrounds political incumbents. It would hasten the arrival of complete accountability that the 24/7 news media has already sought to trigger. In addition, deep-seated partisan divisions are hurdles to meaningful structural change: for example, a lack of consensus on key modernisation committees poses significant hurdles to the design and implementation of new IT projects. There are also understandable concerns about the value of computerised democracy. As Lord Paul Tyler, a proponent of technological change, commented:

> *How do we make the inner workings of government intelligible and meaningful to citizens? How do we avoid the dangers of computerised democracy—so that we don't only hear from a segment of the population? There is a risk that by embracing the web we actually create a narrow alleyway, which becomes crowded and dominated by pressure groups and lobbyists. It can never be a fully democratic system without being fully informed and rooted in meaningful engagement with all citizens.*

In practice, therefore, the conversion of government into a more open, transparent and navigable form is still a distant panacea—but one which, incrementally at least, will help to fuel the next generation of digital news media. The efficacy of an open government would also depend upon an informed and engaged citizenry. For this reason, our third and final recommendation relates to the very root of news consumption—that is, the skills, discernment and experience of the news consumer. If they are to make informed decisions, consumers will need to be able to consciously navigate the noise of the web in general and the expansive news agenda in particular.

There is considerable value, therefore, in new forms of digital media literacy. As we have suggested, the digital revolution heralds an abundance of choice but a scarcity of attention. In the younger generation especially, attention and time are increasingly focused on sites of sociability and fantasy, not sites of news. The transition from mass media to individually customised media is characterised by civic as well as commercial shortcomings. In part, the media is simply responding to a broader and ongoing process of fragmentation and individualisation amongst the audience.

To mitigate the civic damage of that process, we believe it is worth considering the educational routes that may foster a more informed and democratically engaged generation of citizens, who are equipped to comprehend, consciously navigate and critically evaluate not just the output of the converged news media, but also the variety of quasi-news material emanating from government and other bodies such as charities, NGOs and the public relations industry. If 'broadband is becoming the engine of the UK's collective mind and its economy', as Lord Stephen Carter recently commented, then we need to think seriously about new forms of civic education.[149] Indeed, this is a stated priority in Carter's forthcoming *Digital Britain* report.[150]

The hypothetical goals of that education would be two-fold; first, to strengthen, extend and codify the teaching of media literacy at a young age—with the intention of instilling skills at a primary- and secondary-school level related to the reading of the 24/7 multi-channel news, the triangulation of sources and the formulation of informed decisions—and second, to systematically address the transformative impact of digital technology on the relationship between citizens, government and the media—with reference to case studies demonstrating both the wisdom and dangers of networked crowds, for example.

To be sure, the UK's existing educational curriculum (for example, the GCSE qualification in English) does include the teaching of media literacy, albeit in a rudimentary form, which is focused on the mass media rather than the emerging ecology of new media. Depending on the region and examination board, students are taught a range of valuable skills—namely, how to read newspapers, how to compare the editorial voice of different publications, how to differentiate between fact and opinion, how to think critically about the language and claims of a story, and how to assess the impact of a story, both on the reader and on society more broadly.

---

[149] http://www.bbc.co.uk/radio4/factual/mediashow/mediashow_20081105.shtml
[150] http://www.culture.gov.uk/reference_library/media_releases/5548.aspx

Our principal recommendation is that the teaching of media literacy needs to be extended, deepened and upgraded to take into account the distinctive characteristics (and civic challenges) of the digital revolution. The underlying point is that digital media literacy needs to be recognised as a vital part of contemporary civic society, particularly in light of the dramatic speed and scale of socio-technological change. A potential step forward might be to incorporate this kind of education into broader subject areas. In his recent review of the primary curriculum, for example, Sir Jim Rose suggested that larger 'themes' could replace 'individual subject areas'. As the forthcoming Rose review recognizes, the teaching of digital media literacy (and related ICT skills) is a critical pillar of the future curriculum, particularly for themes such as the understanding of 'English, communication and languages'.[151]

Aside from the economic challenges, the civic value of journalism also depends upon the existence and renewal of an informed and engaged citizenry. By investing in digital media literacy, we may be able to offset the structural dangers of the web—and in particular, encourage the kind of informed news reading that will limit a descent into customised echo chambers.

As a society, our view of the world is changing. Over time, we are steadily abandoning the scarcity and linearity of mass media channels for the abundance and interactivity of new media channels. Eventually, all of the information that shapes our decisions, perceptions and fears about the world will be funnelled through some form of digital platform. As we have demonstrated in this report, there are reasons for concern and optimism during this period of transition. In the short term, the craft and economics of professional journalism will continue to morph in new, unexpected directions—some of which will compromise the quality and availability of public interest news. In the longer term, there is scope for various forms of intervention by government, by media businesses, and even by citizens themselves. The digital revolution may spell the end of the mass media age, but it also marks the dawn of a more participatory media age, which promises both commercial and civic dynamism.

---

[151] http://www.dcsf.gov.uk/primarycurriculumreview/

Acknowledgements

I would like to thank the Reuters Institute for inviting me to lead this research and write the report—and in particular, the Joseph Rowntree Reform Trust and David Ure for kindly providing the funds to support a year of research.

The project has been both challenging and stimulating. The breadth of its remit required a variety of fascinating interviews, stretching from the desks of newsrooms to the halls of Westminster. I am extremely grateful to the many people that took the time to speak with our research team throughout 2008. Their advice, insights and experience provide the bedrock of our analysis.

The interviews were planned and conducted with dedication and professionalism by our two researchers, Harriet Cullinan and Kirsten Westlake. From the outset, the project has been guided by a superb advisory group—comprising David Ure (a former executive director of Reuters), Mandy Cormack (a director of the Joseph Rowntree Reform Trust), John Lloyd (the director of journalism at the Reuters Institute and a Contributing Editor of the Financial Times), Geert Linnebank (a Trustee of the Thomson Reuters Foundation and former Editor-in-Chief of Reuters) and Patrick Barwise (Emeritus Professor of Management and Marketing at London Business School).

We were also fortunate to have the support of a wider reference group of experts, which included Vanessia Liu and Phillip Natterman of McKinsey, Lucy Hadfield of Crucible Partners, Lord Clive Soley of Hammersmith, Martin Moore of the Media Standards Trust, Stewart Purvis of Ofcom, and David Levy of the Said Business School and now Director of the Reuters Institute.

Finally, a disclaimer—the findings of the report (including any errors or omissions) remain the sole responsibility of the author and the wider research team. The views expressed should not be attributed to the Institute, the University or the various organisations and individuals that we consulted in the course of the research.

Interviewees

Jay Adelson (Chief Executive Officer, Digg News)
Tony Ageh (Controller, Internet, BBC)
Helen Alexander (former Chief Executive Officer, Economist Group)
Patrick Barwise (Professor, London Business School)
Emily Bell (Director of Digital Content, *Guardian*)
Tim Brooks (Managing Director, Guardian News & Media)
Mark Byford (Deputy Director-General, BBC)
Kenny Campbell (Editor, *Metro*)
Hugh Carnegy (Executive Editor, *Financial Times*)
Rt Hon. Charles Clarke (MP)
Shelby Coffey (former Editor, *Los Angeles Times*)
Josh Cohen (Project Manager, News, Google)
James Curran (Professor, Goldsmiths University)
John Cushing (Deputy Programme Director, News, Global Radio)
Iain Dale (Author and Conservative blogger)
Mark Damazer (Controller, BBC Radio 4)
Jeremy Dear (General Secretary, National Union of Journalists)
Robin Esser (Executive Managing Editor, *Daily Mail*)
Natalie Fenton (Reader and Co-Director, Media Research Programme,
    Goldsmiths University)
Steve Folwell (Head of Strategy, Guardian Media Group)
Daniel Franklin (Executive Editor, *The Economist*)
Des Freedman (Media Research Programme, Goldsmiths University)
Katie Ghose (Director, British Institute of Human Rights)
John Glover (Senior Programme Executive, Ofcom)
Jim Gray (Editor, Channel 4 News)
Roy Greenslade (Professor of Journalism, City University)
Sebastian Grigg (Head of UK Investment Banking, Credit Suisse)
Lucy Hadfield (Managing Partner, Crucible Partners)
Andy Harrop (Head of Policy, Age Concern)
Georgina Henry (Executive Editor, Comment is Free, *Guardian*)
Jules Heynes (Director of Content and Marketing, Media Link)
Paul Hood (Head of Digital, Trinity Mirror)
Peter Horrocks (Head of the Newsroom, BBC)
Jon Hughes (Managing Director of Golin Harris)
Ian Hunter (Managing Editor, Internet, BBC)
Sir Simon Jenkins (Columnist, *Guardian* and *The Times*)
Sir Peter Job (former Chief Executive Officer, Reuters)

Liz Lewis Jones (Director, Chartered Institute of Public Relations)
David Kermode (Editor, Channel 5 News)
Kate Koch (Chief Financial Officer, Financial Times Group)
Richard Lambert (Chief Executive Officer, Confederation of British Industry)
Vanessa Liu (McKinsey & Co.)
John Lloyd (Assistant Managing Editor, *Daily Telegraph*)
Douglas McCabe (Analyst, Enders Analysis)
Gavin MacFadyean (Director, Centre for Investigative Journalism, City University)
Christopher McKane (Deputy Managing Editor, *The Times*)
David Mannion (Editor, ITV News)
Kris Mansson (Chief Executive Officer, Silo Breaker)
Iain Martin (Associate Editor of Comment, *Daily Telegraph*)
Adrian Monck (Professor of Journalism, City University)
Martin Moore (Director, Media Standards Trust)
Phillip Natterman (McKinsey & Co.)
Dominic Nutt (Head of News, Save the Children)
John Perkins (Managing Director, Independent Radio News)
Steve Perkins (Head of Content Policy, Ofcom)
Robert Picard (Director, Media Management and Transformation Centre, Jönköping International Business School)
Michael Prescott (Managing Director, Corporate Communications, Weber Shandwick)
Stewart Purvis (Content and Standards Partner, Ofcom)
Peter Riddell (Chair of the Hansard Society)
John Ridding (Chief Executive Officer, *Financial Times*)
Ed Roussel (Digital Editor, Telegraph Media Group)
Alan Rusbridger (Editor, *Guardian*)
John Ryley (Head of News, Sky News)
Charles Sinclair (former Chief Executive Officer, Associated Newspapers)
Lord Clive Soley of Hammersmith
Anne Spackman (Head of Times Online)
Alex Thompson (Anchor, Channel 4 News)
Tim Toulmin (Director, Press Complaints Commission)
Lord Paul Tyler of Linkinhorne
Fran Unsworth (Head of Newsgathering, BBC)
Jimmy Wales (Founder and Chief Executive Officer, Wikimedia)
Neil Wallis (Executive Editor, *News of the World*)

Simon Walker (Chief Executive Officer, British Venture Capital
    Association)
Roland Watson (Head of News, *The Times*)
John Wellman (Deputy Head of News, *The Times*)
Mark Wood (Chief Executive Officer, ITN)
Simon Wren (Head of Press, UK Home Office)

Suggested reading

Beckett, C. (2008) *Super Media: Saving Journalism So it Can Save the
    World* (Blackwell).
Benkler, Y. (2006) *The Wealth of Networks: How Social Production Transforms
    Markets and Freedom* (Yale University Press).
Berners-Lee, T. (2000) *Weaving the Web: The Original Design and Ultimate
    Destiny of the World Wide Web* (Collins).
Bollier, D. (2009) *Viral Spiral: How the Commoners Built a Digital Republic
    of their Own* (New Press).
Carr, N. (2008) *The Big Switch: Rewiring the World, from Edison to Google*
    (W. W. Norton).
Clippinger, J. H. (2007) *A Crowd of One: The Future of Individual Identity*
    (Public Affairs).
Davies, N. (2008) *Flat Earth News* (Random House).
Gardam, T. and Levy, D. (2008) *The Price of Plurality: Choice, Diversity
    and Broadcasting Institutions in the Digital Age* (Reuters Institute).
Goldacre, B. (2008) *Bad Science* (Fourth Estate).
Jarvis, J. (2009) *What Would Google Do?* (Collins).
Jenkins, H. (2006) *Convergence Culture: When Old and New Media Collide*
    (New York University Press).
Keen, A. (2007) *The Cult of the Amateur: How Today's Internet is Killing
    our Culture and Assaulting our Economy* (Nicholas Brealey).
Leadbeater, C. (2008) *We-Think* (Profile Books).
Lessig, L. (2008) *Remix: Making Art and Commerce Thrive in the Hybrid
    Economy* (Penguin).
Lloyd, J. (2004) *What the Media are Doing to our Politics* (Constable).
Schwartz, B. (2004) *The Paradox of Choice: Why More is Less* (Harper
    Collins).
Sunstein, C.R. (2006) *Infotopia: How Many Minds Produce Knowledge*
    (Oxford University Press).
Weinberger, D. (2008) *Everything is Miscellaneous: The Power of the New
    Digital Disorder* (Holt).